UNLEASHED

HOW TO TURN YOUR MESSAGE INTO IMPACT

UNLEASHED

HOW TO TURN YOUR MESSAGE INTO IMPACT

MARTIJN VAN TILBORGH

INSPIRE

PREFACE

I've been blessed beyond measure. Looking back on my life's journey, I'm amazed at what God has done. At 44 years of age, I'm only getting started. However, even if it were all to stop here, I can truly join Mary Magdalene in her song to the Lord: "He who is mighty has done great things for me!" (Luke 1:49).

Over the course of the last four decades, my career path has been diverse—one could argue it has been fragmented. As a young teenager, I took my first job as a leek planter. Thankfully, that was short-lived. After that, I shelved product in the grocery store, and became a dishwasher at a local restaurant. I decided to skip college and join the Dutch army (which was kind of a joke). Then, I became a window cleaner. After this, I worked in information technology and customer service.

I've been successful in sales, both nationally and internationally. I've worked in full-time ministry. I've helped plant several churches, and have preached in nations around the world. Between my twenties and thirties, I lived on three different continents. The list goes on and on.

My journey has now brought me into what I call my "sweet spot," where I've been for the last decade. I live the life I love. I work with some of the most amazing leaders around the country, helping them with strategic marketing, effective communication, and selling products.

I wrote this book for leaders, entrepreneurs, ministers, and influencers who are serious about leveraging their message and influence, reaching more people effectively, and making money while we're at it. Does this sound too good to be true? I don't think it is. In fact, I'm going to show you exactly how to do it.

The process and principles outlined here are simple. Everybody can put them into practice. But just because it's simple doesn't mean it will come easily. Reaching people effectively will require effort, commitment, and determination. It will require being "unreasonable" in the context of traditional, established methods. But those who decide to trust the process are destined to experience the power of the principles in this message.

Another thing you need to understand before reading this book: this is not a get-rich-quick scheme. There are no shortcuts! This book is written for people who have a burning desire to add value to others. It's all about allowing the gift that God has given you do its work through you, for others. When you're in your "sweet spot," you'll find that financial increase simply becomes a byproduct.

Leaders who are intentional with their gift and message won't only help others. God returns the favor to them. I have seen this happen with those I serve, but I've also discovered it firsthand. God took me—an uneducated Dutch boy, and put me on a path of unprecedented favor and success.

The Bible teaches that when we give, we will be blessed in return: "Give, and it will be given to you. A good measure, pressed down, shaken together and running over, will be poured into your lap" (Luke 6:38). I'm not talking about the offering plate, though there is nothing wrong with tithing. I'm talking about giving to those who have been entrusted to you.

Consider this thought: You are a gift sent by God to the world.

You are a gift when you add value to others. You are a gift when you pour into others expecting nothing in return. God promises to give something back to you: a good measure, pressed down, shaken together and running over!

In this book, we will explore an incredible opportunity to bring your message to market effectively. I will show you the concepts, strategies, and practical actions that have helped others reach multitudes with their content, as well as generate millions of dollars in sales.

I pray that this book helps you discover uncharted territory. I pray that it inspires you to do things in new ways, and to discover your unique value proposition to the world. My hope is that, after you read this book, you'll become an agent of change in a world that pressures us to adapt to the status quo.

You've been given a message, a force given to you to change the world around you.

In this book I'll teach you principles and ideas that will help you to get unleashed, so you can become a blessing to others (as well as yourself).

I pray that you will become unleashed!

CONTENTS

INTRODUCTION

One thing I've discovered in my life is that the abundance of God is a lot bigger than we think.

If you've grown up in the church world like me, I'm sure you've heard statements like this. It's something we embrace on a theological and intellectual level, simply because the Bible tells us so. We've heard sermons, read books, and we've memorized the fact that God's plan is to prosper us, to provide us with a future and a hope (Jeremiah 29:11).

More often than not, however, our current reality doesn't match up with our beliefs. There seems to be a major discrepancy between what we accept theologically and what we experience daily.

Pause for a minute and really reflect on what the Bible tells us in Ephesians 3:20: "Now to him who is able to do immeasurably more than all we ask or imagine, according to his power that is at work within us…"

For just one moment, think about what you've asked Him to do over the course of your life. Think about what you've imagined. Picture the most outrageous and exciting thing that you can fathom.

Got it?

Now think about what this Scripture is really telling us! It says that the very thing you just pictured is absolutely nothing compared to what God has for you. In fact, you can't even measure how much more He has for you.

I don't know about you, but that gets me excited.

So why is it that we so easily settle for second-best? Why does it seem natural to be okay with our current reality, while God says, "No! What I have is so much better!"? The mind has an unique ability to play tricks on us. Your mind has the power to make you believe that your current state of life is acceptable, even though you know better.

Remember the story of the Israelites approaching the river Jordan? They were about to experience the promise God had been talking about for their entire lives. It was a pivotal time. The Israelites had the chance to transition from "just enough" into the full manifestation of everything God had for them. You can read the full story in Numbers chapter 13-14.

The tragic part of this story is that a full generation of believers accepted the lie that all God's destiny for them was, in fact, not for them. Can you imagine that? A whole generation of people somehow settled for second-best.

To make matters worse, their decision impacted the next generation, as well. It was one thing for them to decide God's plan wasn't for them. But what they didn't realize was that this rejection caused their children to suffer, as well!

In Numbers 14:33, we see the following word from God: "Your children will be shepherds here for forty years, suffering for your unfaithfulness, until the last of your bodies lies in the wilderness."

This portion of Scripture refers to those 20 years or younger at the time. The next generation had to suffer because of the unfaithfulness of the older generation. As a result, they became shepherds in the wilderness.

Let that sink in for a moment. Because of the decisions of others—the decisions their fathers made—this next generation became something they were never supposed to be. This wasn't for a short while as they were going through a "life transition." No—for forty long years, they lived a life they were never supposed to live.

Remember, the Israelites were destined to live life on the other side of the Jordan. They would inherit a piece of land that had "their name written on it." Instead, they were stuck wandering in the wilderness, going nowhere, doing what they were never supposed to do.

What a tragedy!

Let's stand in their shoes for a moment. Imagine a world where you see people all around you taking their hopes and dreams into their graves. You, yourself, are settling for a life on the wrong side of the river, unfulfilled and untrue to who you were really created to be. Over an extended period of time, this will break your spirit. Before long, you will accept "the truth" that being a "shepherd in the wilderness" is simply what life is. Slowly but surely, you'll embrace a life of mediocrity. Your dreams and hopes will slowly die.

We go through religious motions, saying the right things, and pretending we're living the life God wants for us, because facing the truth is unbearable. It's simply too painful to accept our reality.

What reality, you ask? The reality that we feel unfulfilled; the reality that we hate what we do every day; the reality that we're stuck in a rat race, trying to keep up with everyone else around us; the reality of barely having enough, and needing miracle after miracle to survive the wilderness.

This book is about changing our reality. It's about breaking free from what keeps us stuck in the past. It's about stripping away old mindsets that hold you back. It's about helping you transition into the fullness and abundance that God has for you. To do that, we need to be a bit unreasonable. We need to adapt our reality. We need to dream bigger than we've dared to dream in the past.

May the blessing of the Lord be your strength as you discover new realities that will help you live the abundant life He has for you. Let's not settle for mediocrity. Let's open our minds and spirits, and let God inspire us in ways He's never inspired us before!

CHAPTER 1

THIS STUFF IS REAL

In 2006, I moved to the United States. My family of five and I had been missionaries in South Africa for almost 3 years when we felt God direct us to move to the U.S. We arrived with just our suitcases—no money in our pockets. My in-laws lived in Orlando, Florida, at the time, which made it an easy decision to move there. Because of our lack of finances, moving into the in-laws' spare bedrooms was our only logical option.

During the next two years, I travelled and preached while my wife, Amy, worked as an executive assistant at a media company. To say we were struggling financially is an understatement. Yes, I was traveling and preaching several times a month, but the occasional $143 love offering and well intended thank-you card (sometimes accompanied by a bar of chocolate) wasn't able to support our family. It was a frustrating time, to say the least.

Before long, we found ourselves in a crazy amount of debt. I wasn't aware of how bad our situation was until, one day, I decided to add up all the credit card balances. They amounted to sixty thousand dollars.

My heart stopped. I freaked out.

Our $35K annual household income was definitely not enough to get us out of this situation. Even Dave Ramsey couldn't save me now. To make matters worse, I discovered that, with our current lifestyle, our debt was increasing by hundreds of dollars every single month.

I was scared. Stressed. I didn't know what to do. I felt like a failure. What was I doing wrong? I was frustrated with God, myself, and the situation. How was this possible? Why did I end up in this hopeless situation? I would lay awake at night with a pit in my stomach, not knowing how we would ever get out of this mess.

I thought I'd done exactly what God had asked me to do, and yet my life was a mess. I was stuck and going nowhere fast.

A PORSCHE AND A JAGUAR

At the risk of being misunderstood and labeled as someone who is in business for the wrong reasons, I want to share two distinct memories I have from this difficult season of my life.

One day, I was standing outside of my in-laws house as the neighbor drove up in his brand new, metallic blue Porsche Cayenne. It was so shiny. It was one of the most beautiful cars I had ever seen.

Wow! I was so impressed with this incredible vehicle that parked itself inside of the neighbors' garage. So close, yet so unreachable!

I was truly happy for the neighbor. For a moment, I caught myself experiencing a glimmer of hope that maybe someday, somehow, I might be able to drive a car like that.

When I caught myself, I quickly killed that thought. *Don't be so ridiculous. A car like that is not for people like us. It will never happen! Don't be so stupid!*

A few weeks later, I had a similar experience. I visited Universal City Walk in Orlando, which is the free area of the Universal Studios theme parks where people go to eat, go to the movies, and have fun. Those who have visited know that there are two ways to park at Universal City Walk. You can park where the poor people park and walk half a mile, or you can pay $45 and park valet. For obvious reasons, I chose to burn the extra calories.

As I got close to the restaurant area, I passed the valet lot. As I looked over, a brand new, shiny Jaguar turned the corner. What an amazing sight! I couldn't believe how someone could afford a car like that and still have money left to pay for the valet. I'd already mastered the skill of killing my hope of owning a car like that. So, as soon as the thought arose, I made sure it was assassinated immediately.

Let's fast forward a few years ...

I was standing in the driveway of my house, which was located in the same neighborhood where I used to live with my in-laws. The difference between our houses was that mine is much larger. It has a pool and a 3-car garage. The garage door opened as I punch the code into the door opener outside. I looked inside the garage, and as I did, these two memories came back to me. I stared at a brand new Porsche Cayenne and a Jaguar XJL.

It's not like I had been obsessively pursuing these cars. In fact, I'd completely forgotten these memories until that moment. Somehow, I'd suppressed my hope so much that I hadn't even remembered it.

In that moment, reminded of these two memories, I was humbled and touched by what the Lord had done in and through our lives. God had taken me on a journey across the river Jordan, and I hadn't even realized it. He did the impossible. Somehow, subconsciously, when it came time to purchase new cars. I'd chosen to drive these same two models and makes.

God showed me that what I can imagine (even if only for a split second), He can do!

Today, I drive a Maserati—a car much more expensive than the Jaguar. As I write this chapter, my wife is looking to trade in her Cayenne for a brand new one. God doesn't just do what we imagine. He does MORE than we imagine.

CHAPTER 2

IT'S ALL ABOUT STEWARDSHIP

Now, please understand that none of this is about the cars. I've driven plenty of old, beat-up cars in my life. At one point, I drove a Fiat Uno that we purchased for $250. And guess what? I was perfectly happy!

I'm using this illustration to show you this:

- You can live a life you love.
- You can live a life of significance.
- You can live a life where you add value to others.
- You can live a life where you are in the will of God.
- You can live a life that changes the world.
- And you can even make money while you're at it!

In fact, I believe this is the only way to live life. I've come to believe that abundance is the byproduct of stewardship.

WHAT IS STEWARDSHIP?

Remember the parable about stewardship? Let's read it in Matthew 25:14-29:

"For the kingdom of heaven is like a man traveling to a far country, who called his own servants and delivered his goods to them. And to one he gave five talents, to another two, and to another one, to each according to his own ability; and immediately he went on a journey. Then he who had received the five talents went and traded with them, and made another five talents. And likewise he who had received two gained two more also. But he who had received one went and dug in the ground, and hid his lord's money. After a long time the lord of those servants came and settled accounts with them.

"So he who had received five talents came and brought five other talents, saying, 'Lord, you delivered to me five talents; look, I have gained five more talents besides them.' His lord said to him, 'Well done, good and faithful servant; you were faithful over a few things, I will make you ruler over many things. Enter into the joy of your lord.' He also who had received two talents came and said, 'Lord, you delivered to me two talents; look, I have gained two more talents besides them.' His lord said to him, 'Well done, good and faithful servant; you have been faithful over a

few things, I will make you ruler over many things. Enter into the joy of your lord.'

"Then he who had received the one talent came and said, 'Lord, I knew you to be a hard man, reaping where you have not sown, and gathering where you have not scattered seed. And I was afraid, and went and hid your talent in the ground. Look, there you have what is yours.'

"But his lord answered and said to him, 'You wicked and lazy servant, you knew that I reap where I have not sown, and gather where I have not scattered seed. So you ought to have deposited my money with the bankers, and at my coming I would have received back my own with interest. So take the talent from him, and give it to him who has ten talents.

"'For to everyone who has, more will be given, and he will have abundance; but from him who does not have, even what he has will be taken away.'"

The message of this parable is simple:

1) When God gives us a talent, we're asked to steward it.

2) When we steward the talent, God will multiply it.

3) When we multiply the talent, God is pleased.

4) When God is pleased, He takes talents from others whom He's not pleased with and gives us even more!

Simple, right? Now, the word "talent" has two dimensions. In the dictionary you'll find these two definitions:

1) natural aptitude or skill: e.g. "he possesses more talent than any other player"; synonyms: aptitude, gift, knack, expertise

2) a former weight and unit of currency, used especially by the ancient Romans and Greeks.

In other words, a talent is both a "gift/expertise" and a "currency." Someone's gift is directly tied to their financial situation. As someone's talent multiplies, so does the money. When God gives you a gift and you work your gift for the sake of others, your financial situation will benefit in direct proportion to the increase of your talent.

The problem is that, many times, we're not working within the grace of our given talent. We work hard, but impact few. We toil and sweat, but live a life of lack. The key is to work within the grace of your talent. When you do this, your impact increases as well as your finances. You cannot steward your talent without benefiting financially. Financial abundance is the byproduct of stewarding your talent. Practically, this means you have to know your gift, your message, your talent, before you can properly steward it.

CONTENT MARKETING

My journey (which I'll tell you more about in the chapters to come) led me to help leaders and influencers in the body of Christ identify their message and effectively bring that message to market. It's been a journey that helped me discover my talent and gift to the world; a journey that helped my clients, as well as me personally, make millions of dollars; a journey that taught me a lot of lessons.

If you're an influencer, leader, entrepreneur, or coach, I'd love to share with you what I've discovered along the way. I will share some of the best wisdom I've learned over the last decade. I believe it will help you steward your message effectively, make more money, and, most importantly, impact people effectively with your God-given gift.

Throughout the chapters of this book, I will help you understand the core principles, concepts, ideas, strategies, and processes that have helped me and my clients every day. You'll also learn from my mistakes, which should help you avoid some of the failures I encountered. You can't put a price on that, can you?

The remainder of this book is all about what the secular world calls "content marketing."

Content marketing isn't new. As a matter of fact, it's quite old. Much of what we see God do throughout the Bible is content marketing. He is the world's best content marketer. Let me explain.

God has a message: a gospel. He wants to share it with the world. He is determined to bring His message to market. In order to do so, He needs an engaged audience. Engaging an audience doesn't happen overnight. It requires a comprehensive strategy over an extended period of time.

God's strategy was executed well throughout the Old Testament: it gave His audience context that would allow them to receive His message. This process came at a price, and not without opposition. His execution was done with precision and determination.

The Bible is all about God's content marketing strategy. He wants His message to be received by His target demographic: the world. God realizes His audience isn't ready. The people He's trying to reach need to be engaged, warmed up, and made ready before they can buy into His message.

So we see that God has a lot to teach us about content marketing. As He gives us His unique message, we should learn from Him and put His principles into practice. That's what we'll cover in the upcoming chapters.

CHAPTER 3

THE GREATEST INVENTION OF ALL TIME

What is the greatest invention of all time?

It's hard to answer a question like this. There have been many inventions over the course of history that changed the world as we know it. The discovery of fire in prehistoric days had quite an impact. How about the light bulb? Or when Henry Ford developed his Model-T and changed transportation forever.

If you're as old as me, you remember growing up without a way to communicate with anyone at any time, from any location. How did we live back then?

I don't know how you determined your answer to that question, but I can tell you what I think was a real game-changer: Barbed wire. You read that right! Barbed wire really changed things.

I discovered this on one of my visits to San Antonio, Texas. I had no idea how barbed wire had impacted that city. I learned that, prior to barbed wire, old-school cowboys would jump on their horses in the morning. They would spend all day hunting roaming cattle in the surrounding area. Life was pretty simple: you don't hunt, you don't eat!

Think about the logistics of a living the life of cowboy. Everyday they would need to do the following:

- Saddle their horse
- Ride in search of cattle
- Hunt the cattle until they catch them
- Bring the cattle home (which, depending on where they found them, could take a while)

This wasn't an efficient way of staying fed, but it was the reality of life back then.

Until one day, someone had an amazing idea for something that would change this dynamic. Barbed wire allowed people to fence a piece of property and contain cattle in one place. They would live in one place, eat in one place, and reproduce in one place. In fact, this made it possible to create an entire ecosystem in one place: no hunting required! Cowboys simply had to roll out of bed, pick their cow, and prepare it for dinner! It changed life as they knew it.

Now, what does this have to do with content marketing? Everything!

Most people market like old-school cowboys: they're stuck in inefficiency. These people put in lots of effort to hunt their prey with little to show for it. The concept of barbed wire, to them, might seem just a bit unreasonable. However, permanently changing your trajectory requires an just such a solution.

I'm going to show you how to "raise your own cattle" right where you are. I'm going to teach you how to build an ecosystem that will produce right under your nose. It will require effort; but once momentum is gained, a lot of your processes will run on auto-pilot. It's true! I'm going to prove it to you.

There is a myth that says, "you can make money while you sleep." The only catch is that it's not a myth. For quite a few years now, I go to bed every night, wake up in the morning, and guess what? I made money in my sleep!

I'm aware that this is a big statement. In the next chapter, I'm going to demonstrate that it's possible.

CHAPTER 4

THE BEST WAY TO FISH

We've explored the concept of a cowboy who hunts all day versus a farmer who creates a self-producing ecosystem. Another example that I want to give you revolves around two different ways to fish.

I'm not a big fishing guy. I genuinely dislike it, actually. The idea of standing by the water with a fishing pole all day in hopes of catching a couple of fish is depressing. The return of investment is simply not there, for me. You have one rod; one line; one hook. This means you have the potential of catching, at maximum, one fish at a time. There must be a better way.

In John 21:1-6, Jesus tells his disciples to throw their net on the other side of the boat. This story intrigues me a bit more. It shows that it's actually possible to fish and catch a bunch of them at one time. Still, fishing doesn't really have much of an appeal.

Now, there has been one instance of a fishing method being brought to my attention that did peak my interest. It was a method I stumbled upon while browsing YouTube. I saw the video, got excited, and decided I would love to try it someday. I want to share the video that I watched that day with you, because it accurately depicts what we're trying to do throughout this book.

Below, you'll find a thumbnail of this video as well as a URL that will lead you to it.

Visit **unleashedforimpact.com/videos** to watch this video!

Did you watch it? Isn't that amazing? I didn't know this existed!

Here are a few guys in a boat, simply roaming the river. They have no nets. They have no poles. No hooks. Really, other than the boat itself, they don't have any equipment whatsoever. Doesn't that seem a bit unreasonable to you? However, by simply being on the river, they catch more fish than anyone with a pole would catch in a whole week!

Why am I showing you this? The answer is simple. I'm going to teach you to fish this way. In our case, we're not looking for fish, but for paying clients. It is, in fact, possible to create an environment so magnetic that fish will jump into your boat. You won't need to go out hunting. You won't need to stand alongside the river with a pole all day in hopes of catching one fish. I'll show you how to build an ecosystem that will make fish jump in your boat. I will teach you how to develop an environment that will make people pursue you as if the pursuit were their idea.

Don't believe me? Let me show you!

Visit **unleashedforimpact.com/videos** to watch this video!

I've discussed this idea over and over, but in the beginning, my words were most often received with skepticism. So, one day, I decided to do a live demonstration to mute my skeptics once and for all. The video below will show you a real-time visual of a highly-engaged audience. They have been developed intentionally to the point that they begin pursuing to buy from me.

Isn't this amazing? I hope you enjoyed this demonstration. The truth is, this is not an isolated success story. We've done this over and over again. The principles, concepts and strategies that are outlined in this book have helped me to personally:

- Generate $500K in 40 days from an idea that wasn't yet an actual product. We sold the idea, generated the cash flow, and built the product (which cost us less than 10% in overhead).
- Build a niche database of over 100K leads in less than 3 months.
- Build the largest children's pastors conference in the country in less than one year.
- Produce half a million dollars in revenue by giving away 4500 books.
- Create $30K in sales, in less than 10 days, by selling a $9 product.
- Generate $100K in 5 minutes of a webinar (and double that in the 24 hours following).
- Sell out an event with a capacity of 400 in days, targeting an email list of only 400 addresses.
- Turn a 650-person conference (which, historically, sold $20K in product) into $250K in sales, simply by making some tweaks.

...and much, much more!

This is not an illusion. This stuff is real! Let's open up our minds, and let's jump in.

CHAPTER 5

THE LAST THING YOU NEED IS A WEBSITE!

This is the conclusion I came to after building 200 websites for my clients. I can't believe it took that long to come to this conclusion; once I did, it seemed so obvious.

After my $60K in debt, come-to-Jesus moment, I knew something had to change. Our current household income at the time, coupled with our attempts to save, wasn't enough. I knew I had to make more money somehow.

At the peak of my desperation, the Lord led me to 2 Kings 4:1-7, where we read about the prophet Elisha and a widow:

The wife of a man from the company of the prophets cried out to Elisha, "Your servant my husband is dead, and you know that he revered the Lord. But now his creditor is coming to take my two boys as his slaves."

Elisha replied to her, "How can I help you? Tell me, what do you have in your house?"

"Your servant has nothing there at all," she said, "except a small jar of olive oil."

Elisha said, "Go around and ask all your neighbors for empty jars. Don't ask for just a few. Then go inside and shut the door behind you and your sons. Pour oil into all the jars, and as each is filled, put it to one side."

She left him and shut the door behind her and her sons. They brought the jars to her and she kept pouring. When all the jars were full, she said to her son, "Bring me another one."

But he replied, "There is not a jar left." Then the oil stopped flowing. She went and told the man of God, and he said, "Go, sell the oil and pay your debts. You and your sons can live on what is left.

The widow in the story is in a hopeless situation. Her circumstances have led her onto a path where she accumulates a tremendous amount of debt. The situation is totally hopeless. There simply isn't a way out for her unless God intervenes. And He does!

The prophet asked her a simple question: "Tell me, what do you have in your house?"

This question is profound. It implies that, even in the most desperate situation, there is something "in your house" with which God can move. When Elisha asks the question, the widow is forced to think about the answer. She's pushed to identify the very thing that would become the vehicle of her deliverance.

A small jar of olive oil: something seemingly insignificant became a weapon of war that would lead her to victory, favor, and incredible abundance. It would not only bless her, but also leave a legacy for the next generation.

WHAT'S YOUR OIL?

When I read this story, I heard the Lord ask about my house. What did I have in my house that He could use to multiply? I thought about it long and hard. I'd never had an education. My Dutch army experience wasn't much help on this side of the pond. Really, I didn't see a lot to work with in my house.

Then, I remembered that, several years back, I'd picked up a book at Books-A-Million. I literally read it cover to cover. It was a book on Adobe Photoshop 6. I picked it up from the sales table, because Adobe 7 had come out at the time (for those who don't know what Photoshop is, it's the leading photo editing software on the market). Ninety-percent of the features in Photoshop 7 were the same as Photoshop 6, so it pretty much taught me the basics of graphic design. I'd used this new skill over the previous few years to do some basic graphics for the ministry in which I was involved. They definitely hadn't been award-winning designs, but I knew enough to be dangerous.

Something else came to mind. Several years back, I'd taken a job at a company called New Horizons Computer Learning Centers. With over 300 locations worldwide, New Horizons was the largest IT training company in the world. I had joined the sales team in the city of Utrecht, Netherlands, where they had just opened a new office. I had no experience whatsoever in B2B sales, but for some reason, they thought I was the man for the job. Boy, did I learn a lot. I discovered I was good at this sales thing. Within four months, I had broken two wall of fame sales records. My boss was ecstatic.

As I was thought about these two opportunities, something in me came alive. My mind was spinning. Could it be that this was my "oil"? Photoshop expertise coupled with a sales background?

The excitement took over and turned into what I can only call a supernatural confidence. *This could actually work!* With my sales and graphic design background, I could probably figure out how to build a website. I had no clue how to do it; but if I put my mind to it, surely I could figure it out. I picked up the classified ads and started calling local businesses who appeared to have no online presence. It didn't take long before I'd made my first sale.

One of my first projects was to build a website for a local storage company called Lake Mary Mini Storage. I sold this project for $299. This wasn't going to get me out of my situation, but it was definitely a start. Before long, I had gotten pretty good at web development. Acquiring new business somehow came easily to me. There was never a lack of projects. I had this huge goal that, maybe, someday, I could make $4,000/month building these websites. Deep inside of me, I believed God would multiply my oil.

Four months later I reached my goal. Four months after that, I doubled that goal. A year later, I doubled it again—and again, a year after that. Eventually, I was generating millions of dollars doing business in the digital space.

BILLBOARDS IN THE DESERT

Something interesting happened. As I started to look at the Google analytics of my clients, I discovered that 60-80% of all web traffic to any given website would "bounce." This basically means most people decide to leave a website within 5 seconds of arriving.

This was extremely disturbing to me. By far, the majority of all traffic didn't stay long enough for my clients to tell their stories. Five seconds was not enough for anyone to engage an audience.

In other words, 99% of the websites we built didn't contribute measurably to the company's bottom line results. The thought was depressing. As a company, we were taking in good money from clients who never recouped their investment.

We were in the business of creating "billboards in the desert."

These sites looked all pretty and cool, but nobody cared. Nobody bothered to truly look at them. It didn't take me long to reach the conclusion that websites, in most cases, are a money pit that only takes from businesses—they don't give back.

The question I couldn't get out of my mind was this: "What can I do to retain people long enough that I can tell my story?" In other words, how do I draw people in? What visual and non-visual language do I use? What is the trick? I became obsessed with finding these answers.

HOW TO KEEP PEOPLE ENGAGED FOR MORE THAN 5 SECONDS

People ask three questions when they stumble upon a web page. All three demand an answer. If we fail to answer these questions effectively within five seconds, our audience will bounce.

Now, our audience is probably not aware that they are asking these questions, but on a subconscious level, they are there. The world of the web is fast. How many times do you search something on Google, click a link, and decide in mere seconds that this is not what you're looking for? People are in a rush. They're looking for information and they want it now. There is little patience. If we know what questions to answer, we'll have a significant advantage.

Here are the three questions:

1) Where am I?

This may be obvious to you, but it's not obvious to someone who has never heard about you. You have one chance to make a first impression. There are a multitude of reasons people end up on your page. Whatever the reasons, we have to assume they don't know much about you. We have to master the skill of defining our organization in one sentence. Remember the term "elevator pitch"? This is like that, only shorter. Within seconds, someone has to be able to understand who it is they're dealing with. You can't tell your life story. No time for it. Don't even try. All you need to do is give them enough to satisfy the question, and do so in an engaging way.

2) What can I do here?

Really, the question is, what do *you* want them to do? You create your call to action based on your objective. Don't clutter your page with too many calls to action. Prioritize. Determine what's most important. If you only have one shot, what do you want to ask them? When you ask, show them the value behind that ask. Give them a reason to say yes.

3) Why should I do this with you?

Third-party credibility is important. Anything that adds credibility from the outside builds a foundation of trust and rapport. Build affiliations with organizations who have more name recognition. Get testimonials from those you've helped. Serve in a way to garner five-star reviews of your products and services.

When I started to implement strategy based on my new found understanding, I saw bounce rates drop. It was a good start, but it wasn't the solution to the bigger issue I was trying to solve. How did I create measurable, bottom-line results? It required being known as the guy who helps people generate money (not the guy who takes their money). Even though I was able to retain traffic significantly longer on a web page, this still wasn't enough for people to develop enough trust and desire.

The simple truth is that people are not looking for an opportunity to spend money with anyone. It's going to take more than a visit on a website. There has to be that foundation of trust before people are willing to grab their wallet and swipe that card.

AUDIENCE DEVELOPMENT AND DATA BUILDING

Back in the early days of the internet, websites were developed to broadcast information. If I wanted information, I simply visited a website in hopes of finding it. It was based on one-way communication. The website would talk to the visitor. The visitor wouldn't talk back.

In today's world, the internet is all about relationship—connection. Websites only play a small part, as the internet is much larger than websites (more on this later).

I discovered that, if I wanted to further my conversation after people leave my web page, I needed to establish some sort of connection that would allow me to do so. The moment someone hit my page should be the beginning of a relationship that continues after they leave.

My main objective was to put myself in the driver's seat: to be in a position where I could further the conversation on my terms. I no longer wanted to be dependent on people coming to me. I wanted to go to them whenever I desired. The only way that would be possible was if I extracted information from visitors that allowed me to talk to them after they had left.

In today's world, information-gathering is accomplished in many different ways. There are multitudes of platforms that allow me to build an audience. I can talk to that audience whenever I want, without being dependent on them. It puts me in charge.

Email marketing remains one of the most effective communications. At the time I discovered these principles, I was focused mostly on email database building and marketing. I decided to forget about websites altogether, and focus on landing pages with data assimilation. I built singular web pages with one objective: which was to build my audience database. We developed incredible strategies to optimize our conversion rates on these pages. We saw conversation rates of up to 82%, meaning that, out of every 100 people visiting our page, 82 would end up in our database. Pretty incredible.

LIFE CYCLE MARKETING

I started working with prominent organizations around the country to help them strategize and develop audiences in the same way. We helped many of them triple—or quadruple—their databases in a short time. Database building became our game.

It didn't take long for me to realize that, if you don't know how to further the conversation with new audiences, it doesn't really matter how much data you accumulate. Some of the biggest success stories we had still didn't have the desired bottom-line results. We were unable to engage our newfound audience.

In one such case, I helped a client build a database from scratch to over 100K in just a few months. We didn't use any advertising dollars; it was accomplished simply by leveraging existing influence. However, when it came time to sell to this audience, the results were far below where they should have been. I realized, painfully, that "the perfect customer" never walks in the door as the perfect customer. They are developed over time. Nobody comes into your database ready to buy.

For example: Let's look at your perfect customer. Let's call him Johnny. Johnny has been a client for years. He didn't just buy from you once. He bought from you over and over again. Not only that, but Johnny also increased the frequency with which he bought, as well as his level of financial engagement. To top it off, he's is telling all his friends about his experience as he buys from you, and talking about it on social media.

We wish everybody could be like Johnny. Right? They can be!

The truth is that Johnny was developed over time. If we identify Johnny's customer journey and pinpoint what made him into Johnny, we can reverse-engineer the process. We can expose other leads to those same circumstances.

What turned Johnny from a cold lead into a raving fan? There were stepping stones along the way. It's important to map out your sales cycle, and identify the stepping stones one needs to take in order for a lead to move deeper into the cycle. Everything has a cycle. You can't shortcut the process; it requires patience.

If I know what turned Johnny into Johnny, I can engineer a process that will create more Johnnys. I just need to make sure that my calls to action are reasonable enough for my prospects to answer them. For example, I can't ask someone who just came in cold turkey to refer his friends to me. That doesn't make sense. We have no history yet. This is all common sense, but we all tend to be impatient.

There is a natural process, made up of seven phases, that defines each sales cycle. This process is uniform for any product and any industry. However, you need to be able to apply it to your product, service or organization.

Life cycle marketing is where I landed with my business. I embraced web development, but this time, in the context of the bigger picture. I help experts and leaders develop not only a website, but a comprehensive marketing blueprint tailored to their organization's objective.

Life Cycle Marketing is all about creating a world that will allow you to build an audience, and turn that audience into Johnnys. Believe me, it can be done! I've done it over and over again.

In the next chapter, I'll break down the typical customer life cycle into the seven phases, and help you apply these phases to your brand and product.

CHAPTER 6

LIFE CYCLE MARKETING

How much traditional marketing can you afford before running out of money?

When one truly thinks about this question, you have to admit that it's pretty silly. The whole idea of advertising is to invest money into giving your products exposure. Marketing is supposed to give your sales a positive boost. Any marketing dollar spent should return more than what you invested. I've never understood "marketing budgets"—why would you put more dollars into something that returns fewer dollars?

Marketing is supposed to render a profit. If you have to ask yourself how much marketing you can afford, you're doing something wrong. If you know that every dollar spent will give you two dollars in return, you should try to put as much money into the process as you possibly can.

The problem is that traditional advertising and marketing don't work. They're inefficient, expensive, and typically, not sustainable long-term. They drains your cash flow and will suck you dry. The graph below shows the traditional marketing model most entrepreneurs use to generate more business.

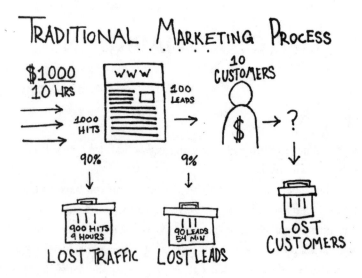

Let me walk you through this model:

Let's say you spend $1,000 and 10 hours of your time to drive traffic to your website. Now, let's say that your time and money generate 1,000 hits on your website. I'm using round numbers to make the math easy. In reality, you will probably spend significantly more money on generating that kind of traffic, through traditional advertising methods.

These 1,000 hits are significant. However, just because they visit your website doesn't mean they're going to buy from you. There are a lot of factors that keep people from buying. The timing might have been wrong. Maybe what you are offering today wasn't something that they needed. Maybe they're waiting for their next paycheck before they can afford it.

In reality, only a small percentage of those that engage with an ad will actually proceed to buy in that moment. But let's say in this example that 10% (I'm pretty optimistic here) are ready to engage with you on some level. Maybe they download a sample product of some sort. Maybe they subscribe to your newsletter. Maybe they even contact you through the contact form on your site.

If you have 10% engage with you, that means 90% of all traffic that you just generated ends up in the garbage. Trash bin number 1 in my graphic will show you where 900 of the people who just visited your website are being dumped.

That's right, they end up in the trash. Why? Because you'll never know who they are. You'll never be able to follow up or engage them again without spending more money.

Put another way, $900 and 9 hours of your time was just thrown in the trash.

Let that sink in for a bit. Somehow, in traditional advertising, we have come to accept the fact that most of what we spend is going to be lost in the process. But that's not all. There's a second trash bin in my graphic. The first trash bin is the largest; it holds most of our lost potential value—specifically our lost traffic.

The second trash bin is called "lost leads."

Just because 10% of the traffic generated is engaging with me on some level doesn't mean they are going to buy from me. I may follow up with my new leads once or twice; but, if they don't buy, we tend to label them "bad leads." Guess where they end up? That's right, in that second trash bin. So let's say 10% (again, pretty optimistic here) of my leads are actually going to convert into paying customers. That means 90% of my leads end up in the garbage.

This means only 1% of my traffic ends up becoming paying customers for me. In other words, $990 of my $1000 spent is now gone forever. We have now effectively generated 10 paying customers.

The question is, what do we do if we want to have 20 paying customers? Within this model, the only answer is to double my spending. Makes sense, right? If $1,000 generated 10 paying customers, then (maybe) $2,000 will create 20 paying customers.

This would probably work, if it wasn't for that third trash bin in the graphic. That bin is called "lost customers." We are losing customers all the time. This is not because people don't like us, or even because they don't like our products. People leave because of apathy. We simply don't develop loyalty among our customers. Then, the first competitor who offers something similar for a better price will take our business from us.

This model doesn't work. It's not sustainable. The big question we need to ask is: how do we recycle the "trash" into something valuable that contributes to our bottom line results? How do we get more return out of our time and money?

The answer is Life Cycle Marketing!

Life cycle marketing considers the customer journey as explained in last chapter. It respects the natural progress of a lead in your sales cycle. Life Cycle Marketing interacts with your leads and clients in context of where they are on their journey of becoming your perfect customers. It has the ability to remove waste from your marking process and redeem the trash in all three of your bins.

I've placed a graphic below to show you the seven phases of the customer life cycle. Let me briefly break down the seven simple phases.

1. DRIVE TRAFFIC

It all starts with driving traffic. This can be done in different ways, some of which don't even cost money. You can turn influence into traffic easily: this is the low-hanging fruit.

Traffic is bigger than a getting hit on your website. It has to do with "attention." Attention is found anywhere you have a voice to a specific audience—online or offline.

If you're reading this book, you are probably an influencer of some sort, or you probably aspire to be one. If you are an influencer on any level, you will have influence to leverage. Moments of influence are created when:

- You speak in front of a group
- Someone visits your website
- Someone checks out your social media page
- You do an interview on a podcast
- You write an article for a magazine or blog
- People read your book
- and many more possible situations!

Basically, any time you are out there influencing people presents you with an unique opportunity to create a long-lasting connection. Yes, paying for traffic or attention is a good idea; but, especially when you are just starting out, it's probably better to look at what you already possess that you can leverage.

One of the greatest tragedies I've seen among high-level influencers is a lack of intentionality in the area of leveraging influence. Some of these leaders speak in front of thousands every week: they have been on television, in front of multitudes, but have never built an audience or database. They created momentary experiences for temporary audiences, but no long-term relationships. What a loss! By failing to do so, many of these leaders have lost millions in potential revenue.

If strategic mechanisms had been put in place to assimilate their audience, they could have furthered the conversation down the road.

2. CAPTURE DATA

By putting simple mechanisms into place, you will convert temporary attention into that long-term relationship. This phase in the customer lifecycle will help you redeem "the trash bin of lost traffic."

I've helped countless clients build massive databases this way. It doesn't require the influencers to do anything different than what they had already been doing. All that's needed is a customized mechanism for each "attention platform." All of these would contribute to building a massive, central database. As you deepen relationships with your audience, this allows you to gather intel and relate to them more effectively over time.

Before I give you practical examples of mechanisms you can create, let me explain what needs to happen if you want people to voluntarily give their identity to you. The reality is that nobody will stand in line to give you their email, phone numbers, address, and so on. They are going to need something in return.

You can get creative in developing a mechanism to get people into your database. The main essential ingredient is this: you have to give people a reason. Nothing is as bad as an opt-in form on your website that says "Receive Newsletter." If you currently have a form like this your website, you've probably found that nobody cares to fill it out. It's offering people more spam than what they are already getting. There has to be an actual value proposition.

An entry into your database requires an actual transaction that involves currency—maybe not money, but definitely an exchange of value. Nobody gives away their personal information without expecting anything in return. You need to create what we call a "lead magnet." This is a free resource that is given in exchange for someone's identity. A lead magnet needs to meet three criteria:

1) It needs to have value

The higher the value, the stronger the magnet. The stronger the magnet, the higher the conversion rate on the page. In other words, if you give away something with a high value, more people will be willing to exchange their identity for it. It's all about supply and demand. The free market is a beautiful thing.

2) It needs to be relevant to your target demographic

We have to make sure the resource we're offering is, in fact, relevant to our intended audience. There is no use offering a skinny, fit person a free resource to help them lose 25 pounds.

3) It has to be relevant to your endgame

There is a saying I use often that goes like this: "If you can't give it away, you can't sell it."

If I try to give away something, and people don't want it, it's impossible for me to sell that same thing to the same people. Your lead magnet should be a resource that allows your target audience to experience a "sample" of what you're trying to sell down the road. In other words, if they like the free sample, they are going to love the thing I'm about to pitch to them.

If that's the case, my free resource pre-qualifies my target audience before I try to sell to them. If your lead magnet meets all 3 criteria, it's guaranteed to work.

Creating lead magnets is fun. You can get innovative, as long as your magnet meets those three criteria. We've given away tons of resources over the years. Some examples are:

- Full training courses
- Printed books published specifically to be a free resource
- Scholarships/financial aid
- Value-based email subscriptions
- Online conferences and summits
- Webinars and online events
- Trial subscriptions
- Curriculum
- Prize giveaways/sweepstakes
- And much, much more …

So, now that you understand how to convince people to voluntarily give their information to you, let me provide a couple of examples of how to practically deploy these mechanisms.

Every platform will need its own custom mechanism. Your mechanism must be compatible with that specific platform and audience. I've worked with a lot of people who have a platform on television. The problem with television is that you don't know who's on the other side of the screen. You are also completely dependent on your viewers to remember when to tune in or record your show. Television is old media, and not where most attention is these days. However, if you're going to be on television, you might as well have a mechanism that converts people into your database.

One way to convert your audience is to create a lead magnet accessible through a text message. People can text a keyword to a certain number that releases the free resource. By displaying that free offer in the lower thirds of your screen, you'll convert a significant volume of data into your database. To do the same trick, you can also use a simple URL with an opt-in page.

If you have a website, you're going to have traffic. When you have traffic, you might as well capture it. Something that has proven effective for me is deploying exit pop-ups. These pop-ups are triggered by your mouse cursor making a motion to leave the website. In other words, you leave your audience alone as long as they're engaged on your website. However, once they've decided to leave, this pop-up serves your lead magnet as an opportunity for them to engage. They were already leaving, so you have nothing to lose. The pop-up offers this person an opportunity get something of value before they disappear forever into cyberspace. Make sense?

All you have to do is to think about your moments of influence. Make a list. Then, think of ways that your audience can interact with a lead magnet with the least amount of friction possible.

Friction is something that could prevent someone from claiming your lead magnet while you are offering the free resource. For example, if your mechanism to claim the lead magnet is calling a number, at the same time as you're speaking at a conference, you create friction. People won't call while they're listening to you speak onstage.

That mechanism is not compatible with the environment of the lead magnet. You need something more like a simple URL they can access on their phone.

Make the list. Get creative. Design a process that allows you to turn traffic into a database.

3. NURTURE LEADS

When you turn traffic into data, it becomes a lead. Once a lead is generated, the nurturing process begins. Depending on what you're trying to sell, multiple touch points are required to create enough rapport and trust for this prospect to spend money with you. A proper nurture process will help you redeem the "trash bin of lost leads."

We'll talk about nurturing a lot more, as it's absolutely crucial to the process. You can only effectively launch a product from a platform of engagement. The nurturing phase is what generates that engagement. When done right, your prospect will be subconsciously brought to a place where he or she pursues *you*.

You want to answer some of their biggest questions and solve some of their most pressing problems, with no strings attached. Adding value develops engagement. Your message offers answers to others' questions. When you demonstrate that message, and prove that it truly helps your prospect, that leads is nurtured.

In the chapters to come, I'll show you exactly how engagement is developed, and give you practical examples on how to do it effectively.

4. CONVERT SALES

Paying customers are the natural result of nurturing leads. The Bible teaches us the following:

"Yet you do not have because you do not ask" (James 4:2). At some point in the process, when enough engagement has been created, you need to ask for the sale. This doesn't always come naturally. Sometimes, we feel asking is too pushy. We don't want to be too aggressive. We figure that, if people want what we have to offer, they'll simply come and get it.

The truth is actually the opposite.

In order to get measurable results in sales, you have to be aggressive. You have to go after your prospects. You have to ask for the sale in order to get it. You can't be afraid that you'll annoy people.

Having said that, in every database, there is always what we call the "bottom 2% of complainers." These people are always annoyed with your sales efforts. They're the ones we're afraid of when we don't want to be aggressive. The danger comes when we listen more to that 2% than to the vast majority of people, who actually want what we have to offer. We can't let complainers dictate our marketing process.

There is only one way to deal with those complainers. Ignore them! Encourage them to leave.

If you try to please the unpleasable, you're embarking on an endless journey—an unwinnable battle. The complainers have never been your customers; they will never be your customers. For whatever reason, complainers ended up in your marketing cycle. However, they have never been your customers, and they never will be.

The people to focus on are the other 98% of your funnel: those who are actually excited about your message. These individuals *want* you to offer them your product. How do I know? Well, remember, they asked for it when they requested your lead magnet. By claiming your free resource, they indicated their interest in buying from you (remember, if you can't give it away, you can't sell it!).

By requesting the free, they indicated interest in your content. If your lead magnet meets all three criteria points as outlined earlier, you can be confident they will love what you're selling.

By the time they are exposed to an effective nurture sequence, they will be ready to buy from you. Subconsciously, they are already begging for your product. We just need to ask them for the sale to push them over the edge.

This "asking" can be aggressive. In fact, any product launch with a specific deadline will require an increased frequency of communication, with increased intensity. Sending 3-4 emails during the 24 hours leading up to when the product offer ends is not too much. In fact, I've repeatedly experienced the power of an aggressive closing in the 24 hours leading up to a deadline. Any limited-time offer, presented over an extended period of time, will double sales if you dare to be aggressive.

If you're offering a product at a special introductory offer over the course of 7 days, you'll sell 50% of your product on day 7.

Now, of course, you need effective copy in your emails to do so; but when done right, you'll see that this is true. The people in your database are all wired differently. People respond differently to different psychological triggers. Most product launches that we do usually end with an aggressive *Gain, Logic, Fear* campaign that triggers different psychological light switches. These switches make people want to buy from you, *now*! Let's take a look at each step in this campaign in a little more detail.

Gain

Some people are triggered by what they can gain from something. If I can show them that their life will be better after they purchase my product, chances are they'll buy from me. I can write sales copy for this type of person: I simply paint the picture of my prospect's future experience that will allow him to see how his life will be enhanced. I also show him the value of buying *now* as opposed to later. For this, I may focus on an expiring discount, or bonus content available if he decides to buy today.

Logic

Other people are triggered by logic. If I can show these people that they are already spending this money in different ways, or that spending this money will actually pay for itself based on the results, I can build a case using logic to push them to the point of sale. If I show Logic people, by logic, that they truly want and need what I have to offer, even better. If I add urgency by showing them that my offer expires at midnight, again, logic will tell them it's better to buy now as opposed to tomorrow, when they'll end up paying more.

Fear

This is probably the most powerful trigger. Most people suffer from what we call FOMO (fear of missing out). If I can show people that "thousands of others are already benefiting from this amazing product offer that's going to expire tonight," I can scare them into FOMO.

It amazes me, every time I send out an email focusing on fear—even hours before an offer expires—how well it does.

All of this to say, don't be afraid to ask for the sale. Convert your leads into paying customers.

5. DELIVER AND WOW!

Most marketers tend to go after new prospects as soon as a sale is made. This is a big mistake. You've just spent all this time and energy to develop enough trust for someone to buy from you, and the moment they do, you start focusing on others. When somebody becomes a first time buyer, you need to make sure their experience is absolutely phenomenal. There's nothing more powerful to your marketing process than a satisfied, raving customer in your database.

We have to make sure we deliver our products with excellence. In fact, we need to WOW them by going the extra mile. Why is this so important? Because, without it, I can't move into phases 6 and 7.

One story that I often share is about a marketing expert I follow online. In one of his campaigns, he offered me a video resource that I could purchase for $300. In this video, he told me that he would teach me "15 different ways to pitch the same product without being annoying."

This was a 40-minute video—a recorded keynote of him speaking at an event. It wasn't even produced to be a product. I couldn't believe that I was actually considering spending $300 on a repurposed video with very low production value. However, as a marketer, I really wanted to know these 15 angles that I could use in my sales process.

So, I sucked it up and put my credit card number in the order form. Deep down inside, I was actually annoyed—with him, but also with myself. I tried to forget about it. When I received my confirmation email, with access details for my product, I quickly logged in. To my surprise, I didn't find one video, but three. The first video was only a minute or so long. I quickly clicked on it.

The marketing expert talked in front of a camera, explaining how he'd "tricked me" into believing I was only purchasing one video from him. Then, he proceeded to explain that, in addition to giving me "15 different ways to pitch the same product without being annoying," he was also giving me a training video on "17 psychological light switches that make people want to buy from you."

Man, I couldn't believe it. What I'd just purchased had doubled in value. The feeling of being annoyed instantly left me. Instead of viewing him as a crook, I now felt I *owed* him. It was the weirdest thing. The funny thing is that he probably didn't lose any sales by not including the second training in his original sales pitch. By not including it, he had leverage he could use *after* the point of sales. He really wowed me! So much so that I'm still talking about it. Not only that, but I'm writing about it in this book.

If he had simply told me that, for $300, I would get two training videos, I would not have been wowed. I would have simply purchased it, and never talked about that experience ever again.

Instead, I'm now subconsciously in debt to him. As a result, he built a lot of emotional credit he can use to cash in later on in the customer life cycle.

We need to do the same. We always need to be thinking about ways to go the extra mile. How can we over-deliver every time someone purchases from us? By WOWING my customers, I'm redeeming the "trash bin of lost customers" by developing loyalty. We should never simply deliver what we promised. We should always WOW the customer.

6. UPSELL

Now that we have a happy paying customer, we need to ensure that we maximize this person's potential. How do you get more revenue out of paying customer? The answer is simple:

- You get him to buy again.
- You get him to buy at a higher frequency.
- You get him to buy at a higher price point.

Are you maximizing your customer database? Are you trying to move customers up the ladder of financial engagement by intentionally offering them other products at higher price points? Are you converting your customers from being one-time buyers into long-term subscribers?

If your answer is "no," you'll have to intentionally think through this phase, and develop a strategy to increase the dollar amount of your average customer.

In an upcoming chapter on "packaging," I'll break down how to build an effective product portfolio that allows prospects to engage—with free, with something cheap, with something affordable, with something expensive, and finally, into something exclusive—all without much friction.

7. REFER OTHERS

Remember when I told you that not all advertising has to cost money? Well, there is no better advertising source then your existing customer database. If you create happy, wowed customers who are purchasing from you over and over again, you will have something very powerful that can generate more quality traffic absolutely free.

Simply ask your customer database to refer people in such a way that it creates a solid flow of new traffic into phase one of your customer life cycle.

In most cases you, don't even have to do something to reward them for it (though it might be nice to do so). If you've spent time and energy developing excellent relationships, your customers will likely do you a favor with no strings attached. Traffic generated by your customer database is much higher quality than cold leads generated through paid advertising because. This is because these leads they come from the endorsement of "their friend."

Not focusing on phase seven is a huge mistake. A large part of the traffic needed to keep your life-cycle alive is generated from this phase. Trust the process. Ask your clients to spread the word!

CLOSING THE CUSTOMER LIFE CYCLE

Now that you understand the seven phases of the customer life cycle, you also understand that one-size-fits-all marketing doesn't work.

Everyone who enters your database is in a different phase of the customer journey. For this reason, we need something called "marketing automation," which essentially tailors the process based on where a lead is in your cycle.

It's possible to build a life cycle blueprint and put it 100% on autopilot. In other words, the life cycle you create for your products will always be working—even in your sleep. When someone enters into your funnel, the automated system takes over.

This is done by deploying the technology that allows you to build this blueprint. At the end of this book, I will give you an overview of the tools I use to build environments like this. I'll provide you with links, so you can explore these solutions for yourself. Not all tools and software are for everyone; but I'll help you identify what you need for your specific situation.

CHAPTER 7

BRINGING YOUR MESSAGE TO MARKET

I've said it before, and I'll say it again: bringing your message to market in an effective and profitable way is extremely simple; it's just not easy. It's simple in the sense that literally anyone can do it. It's not easy in the fact that it will require effort, determination and hustle. It will require being unreasonable in the eyes of the traditionalists.

There's a learning curve associated with the world of marketing and communication. Those who commit to it will definitely be able to reap the fruit of it. Before that happens, you have to count the cost. Remember the videos I showed you earlier, of the fish jumping in the boat and the notifications on my phone? Too many times, people look at these results and think this is all quick and easy. The truth is that all of it requires hard work and focus. It's fun to see the end result, but nothing happens automatically. You have to count the cost.

The Bible tells us, "For which of you, intending to build a tower, does not sit down first and count the cost, whether he has enough to finish it— lest, after he has laid the foundation, and is not able to finish, all who see it begin to mock him, saying, 'This man began to build and was not able to finish'?" (Luke 14:28-30).

The fact that you made it this far in the book is an indicator that you're considering building that tower. I'm confident that you can do it.

HOW THE SEVEN STEPS COME TOGETHER

In the next seven chapters, I'm going to break down the process of bringing your message to market in more detail. I'm going to guide you, step by step, and offer practical tools you can use immediately to start building your tower.

Like the customer life cycle, there are seven steps to this process. Over the years, I've followed (and am still following) many different marketing gurus and experts. I've learned a lot from most of them. One thing I found, however, is that many of these individuals focus on only one or two of the seven crucial steps in this process. For example, I've seen incredible marketers focus on branding; they are amazing when it comes to teaching you how to tell your story effectively. I've seen others focus on how to package content effectively to make it consumable. Others focus on the campaign building, or how to create the perfect Facebook ad.

All of these are important; but they cannot be done in isolation. They must be connected to the rest of the process. What I haven't seen is a comprehensive approach that combines all these components into one master plan. The graph below is my attempt to combine these different components into an overview that will, hopefully, help you see the full picture.

I'm not claiming that this is by any means complete. Chances are that I'll fine-tune this process as I continue to learn more. Based on where I am today, this is as complete as it can be.

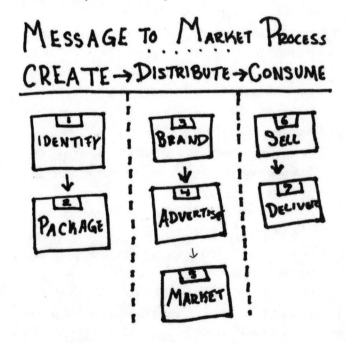

I'M CALLING THIS PROCESS THE "MESSAGE TO MARKET PROCESS"

I've listed each phase, or step, horizontally from left to right in three different categories. Each of the seven phases are connected seamlessly. The danger exists that you might work through each of the coming chapters in isolation. It's extremely important that you don't let that happen. All seven steps are connected. One phase should seamlessly connect and flow over into the next.

In order to help you connect your steps together, I've listed some questions that will help you create continuity.

- Is what I'm currently doing compatible with my overall strategy?
- Does what I'm doing make sense in context of the perfect customer life cycle?
- Is the technology needed for this phase compatible with the technology needed in the other phases?
- How am I innovating throughout this process?
- Am I connecting effectively with my target audience using psychological triggers?
- Are these triggers consistent with what I'm doing throughout other phases?
- How am I developing progressive engagement with my audience in my current phase?

These are just some questions you can ask yourself as you're working through this. In my advanced training I will help you guide through questions like this in more detail, but this should help you get started on your own.

I realize this graph might look a bit overwhelming. I promise that it's a lot simpler than it appears. I'm going to break down each of the seven phases in a simple way, and provide action steps that allow you to immediately apply what you've learned. Let's get started.

OPTIMIZATION VS. INNOVATION

Before we break down each of the seven phases, I feel I need to speak to the role of innovation. Most influencers model their strategy after other successful influencers (especially in the church and ministry world). This isn't a bad thing; however, innovation is essential if we're going to differentiate ourselves.

God is an innovator. When He speaks, He creates things that have never been created. His desire is to do something new, not something that has already been done.

How do I know that? In Isaiah 43:18-19 He says:

Do not remember the former things,
Nor consider the things of old.
Behold, I will do a new thing,
Now it shall spring forth;
Shall you not know it?
I will even make a road in the wilderness
And rivers in the desert.

God declares through Isaiah that He will do something *new*. In order to see that new things spring forth we have to forget "the former things of old."

It's the former things that keep us from innovating. It's easy to look at past successes of other people and model what we do after them. That's not innovation. We call that optimization.

When we read scriptures like the one above, we tend to mystify the "new thing" God is about to do. We think of it as something intangible—unknowable. In reality, it's far simpler.

If we truly believe we're created uniquely by divine design, all we have to do is to become exactly who God created us to be. Then, by God's definition, we are innovators.

Visit **unleashedforimpact.com/videos** to watch this video!

If nobody is exactly like me, and I become who God intends me to be, I'm bringing something new to the table. I'm bringing something that nobody, past or future, will ever bring to the table. There is no other point of reference for what God has called you to do. God does a new thing through us when we become who He created to be. It's as simple as that.

Let's watch a short video that shows the difference between optimization and innovation:

For decades, athletes from all over the world tried to optimize their high jump skills to increase their results. They used the barrel-roll technique as their default method. In the meantime, Dick Fosbury innovated the sport in 1968 when he introduced the Fosbury Flop, which literally took the sport to new heights. Dick Fosbury tapped into something so unique—something that hadn't been done. As believers, we're called to lead, not to follow others' trends.

If we truly believe God created us to be unique, there must be something we can do that's never been done before in exactly the same way. Being aware of the process of innovation is incredibly important. While optimization is powerful and beneficial, it's not going to set us apart. Optimization breeds competition; innovation destroys competition.

Optimization focuses on things like:

- Better technology
- Better copywriting
- Better branding
- Better web design
- Better customer service
- and so on and so forth

Innovation challenges the very framework in which these things are executed, to create an entirely new framework.

Jesus talked about this very thing in Luke 7:28: "For I say to you, among those born of women there is not a greater prophet than John the Baptist; but he who is least in the kingdom of God is greater than he."

This verse is fascinating to me. It speaks about two paradigms:

1) Those born of women

2) Those in the kingdom of God

Jesus contrasts these two "worlds," and shows us the difference between them. In His first example, He speaks about a system in which there can be only one who is the greatest. The culture in this environment is one of competition. John is already the greatest within that category. No one can usurp that #1 position.

Imagine being in an environment like that. You put in effort and hard work, all the while knowing you can never become the greatest. You'll have to settle for second place at best. How discouraging!

In our ministries and churches, we tend to do exactly the same thing the disciples did. We find the greatest one and model our ministries accordingly. These days, that number one spot is taken by a man named Joel Osteen. You may have heard of him. We look at Joel Osteen and make his ministry model the ultimate goal for our ministry. We think, *If I can do half as well as Joel, then I'll be doing great.* This thinking is shallow. We do injustice to ourselves (and God) by thinking like this. This mentality creates hierarchy and ungodly competition. It keeps us mediocre.

We focus on earning more points on the scoreboard, not realizing that the scoreboard we're looking at is referencing how we rank in a world of mediocrity. The best thing that can happen to us within that "system" is that we become the best mediocre versions of ourselves that we can be.

Personally, I would like to be part of the other world Jesus discusses: the world of the Kingdom. That world is much, much bigger. In that world, even the smallest person is bigger than the winner in the other world. A businessman once told me, "If you can't be Number 1 in your category, you need to create a new category for yourself to be Number 1 in." Those are some great words! They made me think about God's categories for us.

Ask yourself this question: How many categories do you think God has for His people? The answer is so simple, yet so hard for us to understand. His portfolio of categories for his children is endless. There is no end to his diversity in the plans and purposes He has for us. By unique, authentic, divine design we all are created different. We are endowed with gifts that have been given to us and to nobody else. Therefore, I need to play a role in the earth that only I can play. Only I can dominate my category, because, by definition, nobody else fits my category. I am one of a kind!

God's kingdom is created to facilitate extreme diversification. Instead of being a vertical hierarchy, it is organized horizontally. This model requires a different way of thinking. Once we become who we are supposed to be in His image, we automatically trump the greatest winners in the inferior carnal world. Isn't that amazing? I sure think so!

OPTIMIZATION	INNOVATION
1 ———— ONLY	
2 ——— ONE	1 1 1 1 1 1 1 1 1
3 ——— CAN	| | | | | | | | |
4 —— BE	
5 ——— THE GREATEST	EVERYONE IS
6 ————	GREAT
7 —— COMPETITION	DIVERSITY
8 ———	
9 —— UNIFORMITY	AUTHENTICITY

It's actually simple. Yet, at the same time, we tend to default back to modeling ourselves according to templates delivered to us by "the greatest." As long as we try to model ourselves after others, we miss the mark.

So, now, with innovation on our mind, I'd like to start breaking down the seven phases of the process we've already identified, beginning with the next chapter. In phase one of the process, we'll talk about identifying the actual message we're trying to bring to market.

Innovation is not just limited to phase one. It's something that needs to be applied throughout all the phases. Throughout each phase, we should ask questions like:

- How can I do this differently?
- How can I do this in a better way?

- Is there a more efficient way of getting this done?
- How can I do this in a way that better represents me?

I can show you countless case studies of unique marketing campaigns that are the result of asking these questions. Challenging the obvious is the best thing that you can do. This doesn't mean the obvious always has to change; but you should at least ask the questions. Don't default to the ways others have done it. Ask questions that force you to innovate, and add a unique spin to your process!

CHAPTER 8

IDENTIFY

Everything starts with identifying your message. What is the unique value proposition God has given you? What value does your calling bring to those around you? Knowing who you are in Christ is the most important, and most difficult part of this process. We start with identity and purpose.

This may sound simple, but many I have worked with struggle to answer these questions. Top-level influencers struggle to identify what they have to offer. Sure, most of them know how to give a generic answer; but this question needs to be answered with precision. What sets you apart from everyone else?

JESUS KNEW HIS IDENTITY

Jesus knew who He was. He knew the specific value He brought to His target audience. We read about it in Luke 4:16-19:

> So He came to Nazareth, where He had been brought up. And as His custom was, He went into the synagogue on the Sabbath day, and stood up to read. And He was handed the book of the prophet Isaiah. And when He had opened the book, He found the place where it was written:
>
> "The Spirit of the Lord is upon Me,
> Because He has anointed Me
> To preach the gospel to the poor;
> He has sent Me to heal the brokenhearted,
> To proclaim liberty to the captives
> And recovery of sight to the blind,
> To set at liberty those who are oppressed;
> To proclaim the acceptable year of the Lord."

Isn't that amazing? Jesus didn't come with a generic, one-size-fits-all message. He knew who He was, and spoke with confidence about what he had to offer to specific people. His message was not abstract. It was practical and clear, tailored toward his target audience.

This is what we can learn from Jesus' ministry:

- Jesus knew He was anointed and called by God with a specific gift. He was able to confidently proclaim who He was.
- He understood His message, and its specific value proposition, as He brought good news, healing, liberty and sight.
- He knew His target audience: the ones who would most benefit from the value He was offering. He knew they were

the poor, the brokenhearted, the captives, the blind, and the oppressed.

Jesus' message was clear. One of His target audiences was the blind. What was His value proposition? You don't have to be blind anymore! Another target demographic was the poor. What was His value proposition to them? You don't have to be poor anymore! Jesus was specific in who He was, who He was trying to reach, and how He was going to help them solve their problems.

What is your unique message and gift? What is the value you have to offer? Who are the people who will most benefit from your message? To whom are you sent?

Jesus knew how to answer those questions. Do you?

THE MANIFOLD WISDOM OF GOD

It's all about knowing who you are, and articulating it in a way helps the people you're called to reach. God chose to give each and every person a measure of that His value to steward. God's distribution strategy is to use us, His body.

The Bible teaches us the following in Ephesians 3:8-11:

To me, who am less than the least of all the saints, this grace was given, that I should preach among the Gentiles the unsearchable riches of Christ, and to make all see what is the fellowship of the mystery, which from the beginning of the ages has been hidden in God who created all things through Jesus Christ; to the intent that now the manifold wisdom of God might be made known by the church to the principalities and powers in the heavenly places, according to the eternal purpose which He accomplished in Christ Jesus our Lord.

This portion of scripture doesn't talk about a "singular" wisdom; it speaks of "manifold" wisdom. There are so many sides to God's creative expression that it's impossible for one human to display them. In fact, collectively as humanity, we still aren't able to define the boundaries of His creative expression: He does more than what we can even think or imagine.

In our limited mindsets, we tend to create ministry templates that allow God to work through us in a limited set of rules we create for Him. Those parameters that we've defined make up only a sliver of the potential spectrum of possibility within God's reality.

Yet when we look at our churches, ministries, projects, and events, they all seem to look the same. Why is this? I like to think God is more creative than what we see happen in churches today. It's because we tend to fall into a deception that keeps us from seeing the full reality of the manifold wisdom of God. We fail to see our unique value proposition. We model after each other instead of trying to figure out who God says we are individually. The devil will make you believe uniformity is a virtue, but it isn't. It may have the appearance of godliness, but it has denied the power thereof.

I discovered this truth several years ago when I was teaching at a Bible college in Aruba, a small island in the Caribbean about forty miles from the coast of Venezuela. I taught for five days. At some point during that week, the church on the island organized a March for Jesus through the main streets of the island. Aruba is small, and has only about 110,000 people, with one major town where most of them live. The island is seven miles, wide and only about three to four miles deep. The churches had decided it would be a great statement of unity to march around the city, holding banners and singing songs about Jesus.

I remember standing by the side of the road as hundreds of people marched through the streets. They all wore red T-shirts, sang the same songs, marched on the same beat, and carried the same smiles on their faces. I guess their goal was to show the love of Jesus through these efforts, in hopes that others would be attracted to this display of "happiness and joy."

Now, I have no doubt that these people marched with a pure heart and an upright motivation. I honestly believe that. Yet, something was terribly off as I watched the crowds walk. It seemed so *forced*. Fake. It felt like it lacked authenticity. Their behavior of walking, singing, and smiling a certain way appeared to have the opposite effect of what they were trying to accomplish.

The random bystander on the street was not attracted by their behavior. In fact, they looked uncomfortable and often looked away in hopes that nobody would hand them one of those balloons or tracts they were carrying. Suddenly, it hit me. God is not looking for uniformity! He's looking for *diversity*. His value for mankind is manifested through the unique value He puts in each of us. He is looking for a unique expression of His manifold wisdom through every individual. Instead of trying to have us all do the same thing, He wants us all to start doing something different!

This was a real eye-opener for me. For so long, I was taught that true unity was created through uniformity. In that moment, I started to see the difference between the two. I realized that the opposite is true. True unity is not accomplished through uniformity; it is accomplished through diversity. Diversity will only manifest fully if each of us find our lane.

So let me ask you again...

What is your gift?

What is your message?

What is your unique value proposition?

What is your lane?

Who are you called to be?

Who are you called to?

Joel 2:7-11 says this:

> *They run like mighty men,*
> *They climb the wall like men of war;*
> *Every one marches in formation,*
> *And they do not break ranks.*
> *They do not push one another;*
> *Every one marches in his own column.*
> *Though they lunge between the weapons,*
> *They are not cut down.*
> *They run to and fro in the city,*
> *They run on the wall;*
> *They climb into the houses,*
> *They enter at the windows like a thief.*
> *The earth quakes before them,*
> *The heavens tremble;*
> *The sun and moon grow dark,*

And the stars diminish their brightness.
The Lord gives voice before His army,
For His camp is very great;
For strong is the One who executes His word.

This scripture describes the army of the Lord the way it is intended to be. No person in this army breaks rank. Nobody pushes one another. Everyone is in their own lane, doing their own unique thing, without competing. And in doing so, they are one. Unity is the result of each individual finding their own place within the army. No rank is the same. No position is equal. It's uniquely designed for each individual to march. And as we march in that unique, authentic way, we become one.

This phase is all about giving birth to the very thing for which God created you.

We don't tend to promote this in our ministries and churches. More often than not, we operate in wineskins, structures, and leadership models that don't facilitate the kind of environment where identification can take place.

THE THREE LEVELS OF REVELATION

There is an interesting story in the Bible, in which Peter converses with Jesus one day. We find it in Matthew chapter 18. Let's read it:

When Jesus came into the region of Caesarea Philippi, He asked
His disciples, saying, "Who do men say that I, the Son of Man,
am?" So they said, "Some say John the Baptist, some Elijah, and
others Jeremiah or one of the prophets." He said to them, "But

who do you say that I am?" Simon Peter answered and said,
"You are the Christ, the Son of the living God." Jesus answered
and said to him, "Blessed are you, Simon Bar-Jonah, for flesh
and blood has not revealed this to you, but My Father who is in
heaven. And I also say to you that you are Peter, and on this rock
I will build My church, and the gates of Hades shall not prevail
against it. (Matthew 16:13-18)

I'd heard this story many times, and thought it was a cool story. However, after hearing it one too many times, I started to get bored. How many times can you listen to the same sermon without getting bored?

My boredom was short-lived after I got a revelation from this portion of scripture which I had never recognized. It forever revolutionized the way I look at things. Let's paraphrase the story a bit as we unpack it. Jesus is sitting down with Peter one day. They are having a conversation. Jesus asks him:

"Hey Peter, tell me, what is the word on the street?"

Peter answers, "What do you mean, Lord?"

Jesus: "Well, who do the people say I am? Tell me, what stories are being told about who I am. What's the word on the street?"

Peter: "Well, actually, there are quite a few stories going around about you, Lord. Some say that you're John the Baptist who came back from the dead. Others say you're Elijah or one of the prophets. I can't really answer that question since there are many, many stories going around from different people expressing different opinions!"

Jesus' question and Peter's answer is what I call a first-level understanding (or revelation), which we all have at some point in our walk with Christ. There's nothing wrong with it. In fact, there is a time in your faith walk when you simply believe what others say about Jesus. When you become a believer, you simply believe what the pastor tells you about Jesus is. There's nothing wrong with that—it's where we all start. But it becomes a problem when we stagnate and stay at that level. There is a higher level of revelation we all need to get to at some point in our walk with the Lord. Let's look at this Level Two revelation next.

Jesus: "Well, Peter, now that you know what other people say, let me ask you another question: Who do you say that I am?"

Wow. The questioning became personal. It no longer matters what others told Peter. It was now up to him to tap into a higher level of understanding, to answer that question for himself.

Peter answers: "You, sir, are the Christ! You are the son of the living God!"

Jesus: "Oh, wow, Peter! I'm impressed. This is some information that you didn't get off the street. This is not something anyone has told you. This is pure revelation from the Father. He Himself must have revealed this to you, because this isn't public information."

Now, remember, when Peter answered this question, it wasn't public knowledge that Jesus was the Son of God. Nobody really knew who Jesus was at that time. The information Peter shared was the result of a supernatural experience with the Father. Peter had been given a revelation from God Himself, showing that Jesus was the Christ, the son of the living God! He didn't read it in the Bible like we do, because there was no Bible as we have it today! Pretty amazing, isn't it? Peter heard from God about who Jesus truly was! This was another level of revelation, far beyond what was heard in the streets. It was supernatural. It was personal. It was a game-changer for Peter.

When Christ is revealed to us on a personal level, that revelation becomes realer than any circumstance and reality around us. When this happens, you can truly start your walk with God.

And that's exactly what it is. You *start* your walk with God. This level cannot be our end goal. It's merely the starting point that puts you on a path to a third level of revelation...a level that no one ever seems to discuss.

You see, most church culture is crafted in order to get people to the second level of revelation. As leaders, we tend to make it our goal to help each person get a supernatural revelation of Jesus. We have come to believe that, once people get to this level, they have arrived. Guess what? It's not true. It's not true at all! It's really only the beginning.

I honestly believe that by making this second-level revelation our primary goal, we distract the church from being truly victorious. Why? Because on this level, we all are equal. Though necessary, this second level of revelation becomes the breeding ground for uniformity if we stay there too long.

The conversation Jesus had with Peter shifted the focus from Jesus to Peter. The first two levels of revelation were about Jesus; however, there was a third level Jesus wanted Peter to grasp that had nothing to do with Jesus. It had everything to do with Peter.

When Peter was ready to receive it, Jesus turned to him and said: "Peter, now that you know what other people are saying about Me, and now that you know, by revelation, who I am, it is time for you to understand something else. Let me tell you who *you* are! You are

Peter, and on this rock I will build My church, and the gates of Hades shall not prevail against it."

Wow. Let's think about this for just a moment. For the first time in his life, Peter had a revelation about who *he* was supposed to be, as Jesus Himself identified him by uttering words of destiny and purpose over his life. Jesus declared the very thing that made Peter unique. He called him Peter (Rock), and with those words, He released a revelation of prophetic destiny over Peter.

It's this third-level revelation that we all need to have. It's this level of understanding that will truly make us all diverse—unique. We have to hear the same words Peter heard that day. The only difference in this third level of revelation is that the words are unique to each of us.

We need to come to a place where Jesus turns to us and says, "Now that you know what others say, and now that you know who I am, let me tell you who *you* are!"

This supernatural revelation will propel us into our unique prophetic destiny. In fact, it's this level of understanding that becomes the foundation of the church, against which the gates of Hades can't prevail.

If we want to truly overthrow the gates of hell, we need to attain this level of revelation. This is where the action happens. On this level, the battle is won. This is the place where everyone in God's army finds his or her lane, position, and rank. It's power in diversity,

Know who you are. Identify the message God has given you. Be confident, demonstrating your unique value through the concise articulation of your message. Know your target audience, and what it is you offer that will help them with specific problems.

Once you answer these questions, you'll be ready for step two. In the next chapter, I'll help you make your message available to your target audience.

CHAPTER 9

PACKAGE

We must begin with the end in mind. We need to define what we're going to sell down the road so we have something to focus on throughout the process. We can do this by taking the information we possess and packaging it into a product portfolio.

As long as your message is only in your head, you are the only one who can consume it. Somehow, you must make it available for others to access. We call this process packaging!

We've already learned that everybody has been given a talent—a gift—a message: something from God, given to you in order to bless others. As an influencer, you possess information others can use to succeed in specific areas of life.

In my own life, I've often discovered that I don't realize what I know until someone asks me a question. Have you ever experienced this? Someone asks you a question, and suddenly, you realize you have the answer! I'm convinced that everyone has information that can help answer others' questions. It's simply a matter of identifying that knowledge, and making it available for consumption.

So much of what we know lies dormant inside of us, waiting to be pulled out. Information is powerful: it has the ability to answer big questions; to solve problems; to educate; to save us years of struggle. However, it is not tangible unless you make it tangible.

Most Christian influencers only think two-dimensionally when it comes to their message. They know how to package it one of two ways:

1) They preach it

2) They write a book about it

That's it. That's the extent of their creativity. If you're not a writer, you're in trouble: all you can do now is preach.

These formats are not ideal. Don't get me wrong—they serve a purpose. You're reading a book right now—obviously, I believe books play an important role in information packaging. The challenge is, books and sermons are limited vehicles. They're not always the most effective in making sure your message reaches its full potential.

Most books, for example, are never read cover to cover. People buy books as souvenirs. They look good on bookshelves. How do I know this? Walk over to the bookshelf in your home. Tell me how many of your books you've read cover to cover.

...Exactly.

Except for maybe a handful of people reading this book, most people have multitudes of books they haven't read fully.

Likewise, sermons are largely only consumed in church. Sure, you can put them on YouTube, or distribute them a podcast. Generally speaking, though, you come to church to consume a sermon. Your message has so much more potential than reaching only those who show up on Sunday morning, right? Limiting your packaging sermons will also limit your capacity to reach people.

From an economic point of view, it gets even worse. Sermons, of course, are free (and should be). Books rarely sell for more than $20—it doesn't matter how life transforming the information is. This is pretty crazy when you think about it.

I've come to the conclusion that many Christian influencers are broke because they haven't packed their information in an innovative and strategic way. If we can make our information available in different formats, we will not only reach more people more effectively—we will also be able to monetize our information exponentially more.

You see, information travels in different ways:

- People read
- People listen
- People watch
- People attend
- People participate

These are all vehicles that allow you to package information. Why limit ourselves to only two specific formats?

Let's say you're a leadership coach. You're writing a 10-chapter book on leadership. Each chapter breaks down an important principle that every leader should know if they're going to grow their organization. As discussed, this book won't sell for more than $20.

This is not a lot of money, compared to the effort it takes to publish the book.

Now, I happen to own a publishing company that helps many authors publish books and bring them to market. Depending on the scope of the project, book publishing can be expensive. It takes a long time. It's not as if you decide one day to write a book, and have it ready within the week. It takes time and money.

Writing a good manuscript, typically, takes months. Then, you edit it. You probably want to do another proofread after that. Next, it need to go to interior design, which lays out the inside of the book. You're going to need a cover designed; if you want the book to stand out, and not "self published" looks, you probably want to pay a designer to do this. Then, you need to create inventory and invest in some stock. Nowadays, with digital printing, you can print books on demand, which allows you to minimize inventory; still, you're going to need to invest in stock before you even sell the first book.

Finally, when you're ready to sell your book, you can only sell it for about $20. It's going to take some effort to recoup your investment. Needless to say, you'll need a lot of effort and sales to get your money back. So again, from a financial point of view, a book is not the most ideal format in which your message can be packaged.

A NEW PACKAGING STRATEGY

Now, take that same 10-chapter book and turn it into a 10-week online journey, in which you provide group coaching for leaders. You market this course as a "10-week coaching experience," which takes place through an online video conference call. Each week, you teach on a chapter from your book, opening the floor for Q&A afterwards. You create a syllabus outlining the course, and coaching questions for each session, to make the material practical for each participant. At the end of the 10 weeks, you issue a certificate to those who have completed the course.

Suddenly, the same content is worth exponentially more. Depending on the status of your expertise, you could potentially charge hundreds of dollars (maybe even thousands!) for this self-same information.

And do you know what's even better? Creating a 10-week course like this takes significantly less labor, time, and money than publishing a book. All I have to do is create an initial outline of my course, and I can already sell it. As long as I'm ready for session one, I'll be good.

I remember working with a business partner on a project like this several years ago. I had worked in the children's ministry space for several years, and I'd developed tremendous influence in that niche. I'd even developed a friendship with one of my clients who was an expert in that market. The problem was, nobody knew who I was.

Now, people always told me there was little money in children's ministry. The truth is that many churches don't make it a priority in their budget. However, I was convinced we would be able to add tremendous value to the community of children's pastors.

I remember pitching a project to my friend: I told him we should create an academy for children's pastors that would be time-flexible, affordable, and 100% online. We'd call it Kidmin Academy. I had observed that there was few training resources of quality available for children's pastors. One would either have to go to an expensive seminary (a viable option for a select few), or...absolutely nothing. Those were their options.

I explained that, if we created an online academy with twelve core modules—if we recruited high-level faculty that could impart valuable wisdom and insight— we'd be creating something people would desperately want.

My friend gave me twelve topics for the modules, and twelve names of potential faculty. The faculty were experts he identified from his own network—one which he'd developed over the years. We blueprinted what this program could look like, and decided that yearly tuition would cost $1599.

We built a website around the idea, as if the program already existed. We developed an advanced marketing strategy to bring it to market. We invested $1500 in a website, and some sweat into the campaign. This entire endeavor was out of the box, but I knew that if we could get 50 students in this new program, we could proceed and build the academy. (If you are ever able to go through some of my advanced training, I break down marketing strategies like this in more detail). Within *five days*, we had 50 students. Within forty days, we had over 400 students: the first Kidmin Academy class. We generated over $500,000 in revenues in forty short days, from an idea that allowed us to sell other people's content.

Can you believe that? That's the power of packaging.

All we had was:

- An idea for a training program
- A website that communicated this idea
- A marketing campaign would sell the idea

The commitment of faculty to deliver content centered around our idea

By now, over 1500 children's ministry leaders have graduated from Kidmin Academy, which has become a multimillion dollar program. It's generated spin-off projects, including Kidmin Nation Mega-Con, the largest children's pastors conference in the country. This conference was simply another way to package information, specifically for children's pastors.

It's not about your book; it's about your message. Your book is simply one of a wide variety of formats you can develop to share that message.

THE ASCENDING VALUE LADDER

When you package your information, you need to create an ascending value ladder. What is an ascending value ladder, you ask? Great question! Allow me to explain.

Most books are published in isolation. If the only product you have to sell is a book, you can't afford not to make money on that book, right? If the book is all you have, the book is your only opportunity. You can't afford to give it away or discount it too much. By doing so, you'll end up losing money instead of making it.

This means there's no "next step" in the sales process. People may engage with your book and give you $20, but that's where it ends.

Then, all you can do is write another book, go back to your same audience, and (hopefully) make another $20 two years from now when you finish publishing that one. Not very effective.

What you need to create is a value ladder—essentially, a portfolio of products that allows you to systematically move your clients up the ladder in a logical, natural way. Your audience's engagement with a product on the lower levels of the ladder will lead them to the next level of financial engagement.

Each product ladder should always begin with something FREE. This is your lead magnet. Next, it moves on to something cheap; then, into something affordable; then, into something more expensive. Finally, the ladder ends with an offer for something exclusive.

Do you know who understands this ladder model well? Your dentist! That's right. Your dentist is an expert in creating ascending value ladders. Remember that direct mail in your mailbox that he sent you for a "FREE CLEANING"? You thought he was an idiot for offering it, so you probably went ahead and made an appointment. After five minutes in his chair, your dentist asks if you're a smoker. You clearly are not a smoker, but are embarrassed by your yellow teeth. He pressures you into a teeth whitening plan that will cost $800.

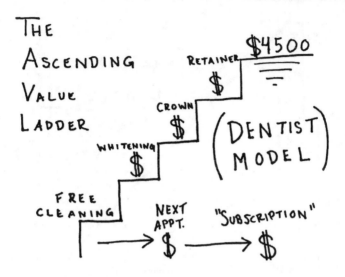

Next, your dentist points out the crack in your back molar. It really needs a crown, or you're eventually going to lose your tooth. Well, you don't want that to happen! So, reluctantly, you agree to the $1500 treatment plan he recommends. What closes the deal is the payment plan he offers—a plan that will ease the pain of the financial commitment it takes to get this treatment completed.

Now, in today's society, if you're lucky, he'll also convince you to get an adult retainer that will straighten those crooked teeth of yours. They've always been like that, but something he says convinces you that it's truly a good thing to finally get them fixed.

You get the point. Before long, you walk out the door with a $4,000 bill. You only came to claim something that was offered to you for free! When you attempt to leave the office, the receptionist will stop you to set up your next appointment six months from now (which you obviously schedule, as any responsible person would do).

Congratulations! You are now part of the dentist's continuity program. Every six months, you can come back and have him sell these services to you all over again!

We need to be like the dentist. We need a ladder like his. If we create it successfully, we won't need to worry about giving away products for free. This will *make* us money, not result in a loss. It seems counterintuitive, but I promise you, it works. Having a ladder removes my book from isolation; now, people who claim my free book become prime candidates to sell to at a higher price point (remember, if you can't give it away for free, you can't sell it!).

As long as enough people convert to those next tiers of financial engagement on my ladder, there isn't a limit to how many free products I can give away. The more I give, the more money I make. It's really a beautiful thing.

So, how can we develop a ladder that will move people from consuming free products into high levels of financial engagement?

It's actually simple. By lowering your price to zero, you are actually maximizing the demand on what you're offering! When you create an ascending value ladder that works, you've basically created a machine that outputs a profit.

THE BROKEN PUBLISHING MODEL

I work with many publishers. Many of them have hired my services to help launch books for their authors. The publishing world hasn't changed much over the last 100 years. Don't get me wrong: the digital age has heavily impacted the way we read books; publishing a book has become increasingly easier, even over the last 20 years. What I mean when I say it hasn't changed is that the actual model of book publishing hasn't changed. Publishers (and most authors) make center their strategy solely around the book, instead of the message. There is no ladder. There is only a book. The main objective, the complete sales model, is to sell as many units as possible at the highest price possible.

Because they can't move beyond the book, they can't afford to discount it, let alone give it away. As a result, it's extremely difficult for publishers to break even. Most "traditional" publishers focus on the first week after a book releases. They try to sell as many books as possible. Those numbers (if recorded by a reporting agency) will count towards rankings that will determine who ends up on the New York Times Best-Seller list.

My point here is that most publishers focus on selling high volume during this first week, and manipulate the reporting system to get rankings that, in reality, don't mean much. They jump through all kind of expensive hoops to maximize their sales early on in the launch process.

I don't know about you, but personally, I'd rather sell 50,000 books over a longer period of time than have a 15,000 initial launch that flatlines after the first week.

One early sales strategy is offering bonus content if readers pre-order the book before it releases. Publishers offer the book at regular pre-sale pricing, but provide a mechanism to claim additional resources for free after customers purchase the book.

The problem is free market enterprise: supply and demand. When you sell your book at regular price, even if you include bonus material, you still aren't maximizing your demand. How do you maximize your demand? By lowering your price, preferably, all the way to zero dollars. You'll find that more people are interested in free than in buying something at regular price. Common sense, right?

Of course, if you don't have other products to offer, you can't afford to give away your book. You'd need to have a ladder in place to compensate for the $10 you'll lose. That's why I decided a long time ago to do away with the traditional sales model (offering the book at regular price, and including free bonus materials for those who purchase early). I decided to flip that funnel! Instead of giving away free stuff along with a regular-price purchase, I prefer to *give away the main product, but charge for the stuff*.

When I give away the book, I'm maximizing the number of people who enter my sales funnel. If the conversion percentages on my value ladder work, there is no limit to how many free books I can give away: the more the better, because the more free books I'm giving away, the more profits I'm making. Then, the only thing I need to worry about is getting more people to claim my free book. My ladder will take care of the rest.

Remember the video with the notifications on my phone? This was a live demonstration of a book funnel/ladder that I did for one of my clients. We gave away 4,500 books for free, and generated half a million dollars in revenue selling the same content in different formats. We built an ascending value ladder that worked!

If you've been to one of my seminars or purchased my advanced training, I show you exactly what I did to accomplish this. It really is simple. Anyone can do it. All you need is a blueprint, and the tools to build your funnel.

CHAPTER 10

DISTRIBUTE YOUR BRAND/MESSAGE

In Romans 10:14, the apostle Paul asks us the following: "How then shall they call on Him in whom they have not believed? And how shall they believe in Him of whom they have not heard? And how shall they hear without a preacher?"

The process Paul defines in this Scripture is God's sales and marketing process as it relates to the Gospel. Let's break it down:

- God's ultimate "sales goal" is for unbelievers to "call on Him"
- In order for that to happen, the Gospel needs to be heard
- In order for the Gospel to be heard, there needs to be a vehicle that will get the word out: a preacher

If we want people to buy into our message, we first need our message to be heard. We need to make sure we have a vehicle that allows us to "preach" our message to our target audience. Let's start with three questions:

- What is the value of my message?
- Who can benefit most from that value?
- Where do I find these people in large numbers?

If I can answer those questions effectively, all I have to do is to share the value of my message in places where my target audience congregates, and I'll be successful. It really is as simple as that.

Questions 1 and 2 are questions you've hopefully already answered in previous chapters. If not, I recommend you go back to chapter 8, about identifying your message, and answer the questions at the end of the chapter.

Question 3 is the most important. Where do you find your people in large numbers? We have to identify the attention of the people we're trying to reach. If I'm able to demonstrate the value of my message in those places, I'll create a connection, develop an audience, and, ultimately, create a strong database.

The platforms where people put attention these days have dramatically shifted. Where do people spend their time? Where are they engaging? Where do they consume content? The answers to these questions used to be television, radio, magazines, conventions, etc. Before the internet, the only way to get in front of your target audience was to spend a lot of money in advertising. Spreading the word was expensive.

These days, it's a lot easier to reach people. Attention has shifted. People don't watch TV the same way. Television ads are overpriced and are underperforming. Anyone who claims TV is still a valid vehicle to reach people with their brand is in denial. Even executives from large ad agencies will come home at night and decide to spend their time watching Netflix or scrolling through their Instagram feed instead of watching the TV they sell to their customers.

If you want to reach people, you have to reach them where they spend time. The good news is that we all have access to those platforms. The best news is that it's free!

People spend massive amounts of time on Facebook, Instagram, Youtube, LinkedIn, Snapchat, blogs, vlogs, podcasts, and other social media platforms. If we want to reach them, we need to talk to them on those platforms, and create content specifically for those ecosystems.

One question I often get asked is, "How do you know what platform to pick? What social platform do I use to get the word out about my brand?" I used to answer that question very differently: I used to tell people to pick their "weapon of war"—one or two platforms that suited their personality the best. I'd advise them to put all of their eggs in those few baskets. Today, I tell people to pick all of the platforms their target audience is using. Chances are that audiences are spending time on all of them, in some capacity.

Just because you're not comfortable with LinkedIn doesn't mean your audience is not spending time on LinkedIn. By not distributing your brand messages on LinkedIn, you're missing an opportunity to reach them. So the answer to the question of what platforms you should leverage is: ALL OF THEM!

Now, obviously, you'll need to be intentional in how you do this. You can't just go around all these networks posting random content and hoping something sticks. As you distribute your brand message, here are some guidelines and golden rules you'll need to follow:

NEVER SELL; ALWAYS ADD VALUE

I know it's tempting. You want to sell your products. But the golden rule of branding is to offer value first. If you want to create a connection and build an audience, offering value is key. If you come across as someone who only wants people's money, you will push people away and they will not engage with you.

Don't worry—in the following chapters, I'll show you how to monetize your efforts down the road. You simply can't be in a hurry. You have to be patient and trust the process.

Offering value first is the best thing you can do to create long term success for your brand. You have to create valuable content, and you have to put it out across different networks and platforms.

People don't buy your products to do you a favor. People buy products for selfish reasons. If you can't demonstrate that what you have to offer is going to help them, people are simply not going to give you money.

Let me tell you a story to illustrate this point. I mentioned before that I own a publishing company. You'd be surprised how many people tell me that God told them their book will be a best-seller. Now, of course, God can do whatever He wants to do; but the reality is that 99.9% of all books don't become best sellers. I've seen countless authors order large inventory of books from me because they believe they're going to sell them. They will order 5,000 books, because God told them it's gonna sell.

However, they fail to understand this very basic principle: People buy stuff for selfish reasons. They want to know what's in it for them before they pull out their credit card.

The number of authors with book boxes piled up in their garage is astounding. The first 50 books are easy: they go to family, friends, neighbors, acquaintances and those who know the author. They buy a book simply because they feel sorry about those boxes in your garage.

The other 4,950 books, however, will need to be sold to strangers. They are not going to feel sorry for you. They are only going to buy your book if you show them value. They want a return on their investment. They want to know how their life is going to be better after reading your book. If you can show them that, you'll be in a good place.

Below is a graphic with three circles. These circles represent three types of communication when it comes to our brand message.

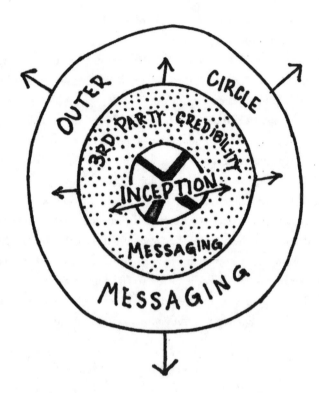

1) The outer circle of messaging is what most people use when it comes to spreading their message. They say something like,

Hey friend! I have a product and it's totally awesome. It's gonna rock your boat. Your life will never be the same again. Everybody likes it, and guess what? It's on sale this week. It's buy one get one free. You should really, really buy it, cause it's really, really good!

What's wrong with this message? Everything!

You're simply tooting your own horn without any evidence. Of course you think your product is awesome—it's your product! Meanwhile, your target audience is wondering who the heck you think you are, and how they are definitely not going to spend money with you, because the risk is way too big.

2) The second circle is a bit better. It's based on third-party credibility, and it goes like this:

Wow, I can't believe how this product has helped me. When I purchased Johnny's product, I didn't think it was going to work, but look at me now. I am seeing all these specific results in my life because of what Johnny did through this product. You should try Johnny's product too, if you want the same results I've experienced!

Much better, of course. I'm no longer tooting my own horn, but I'm using third-party credibility to tell the story on my behalf. The problem is, the potential customer still has to take someone else's word for it. They don't get to experience it on their own. Maybe this testimonial is simply from an actor—maybe they're paid to say this. Your audience doesn't know.

The number of commercials I've seen featuring retired NBA player Shaquille O'Neill is incredible. It seems like he endorses anything that pays him well. I don't know about you, but I'm still skeptical about this type of messaging.

3) The third circle is pretty small, but by far the best. This is the message you should focus on. We call this circle an "inception circle."

If you've watched the movie *Inception*, featuring Leonardo DiCaprio, you know what I am talking about.

In the movie, certain characters are able to implant thoughts into the subconsciousness of others while they sleep. They can enter their dreams and plant ideas; when the sleeping characters wake up, they believe the thoughts are actually theirs. A new reality is formed through inception.

By using this third circle of brand messaging, you'll be able to create a situation where people develop a subconscious desire to start buying from you. They will think that buying from you was actually their idea, instead of yours. How do you accomplish this? The answer is simple: *Never sell; always add value!*

This is the very foundation of creating online engagement. Add value; answer questions; solve problems!

If you're able to do that, with no strings attached, people will begin to trust you as an expert, and desire more of what you have to offer. So the best thing to do when you're distributing content on platforms is to add value.

REPURPOSE TO SCALE

You may be staring at your list of platforms thinking, "How do I create content for all of these? This is going to take too much time!" Sure, it takes effort; but what if I told you that you probably already have the content? Would you believe me?

Most influencers create content; they just don't re-purpose it well. Content needs to packaged in the right format to be compatible with the platform. Let's say you are delivering a keynote at a conference. The keynote is 40 minutes long, and you have the video file. This video file can be used to create content for a multitude of other platforms.

You can post the keynote to your YouTube channel.

You can strip the audio and create a podcast.

You can transcribe a portion and create an article for LinkedIn, or your blog.

You can email that article to your mailing list.

You can identify segments of 59 seconds or less to create short videos for Instagram.

You can pull out a dozen or so one-liners that can be turned into social media graphics to be posted on Facebook, Instagram stories, and so on.

Content doesn't always need to be created. If you look hard enough, you'll find material you've already made, simply by doing what you're already doing.

Now, you need a system that allows you to repurpose that content on the right platforms for your audience. In some of my advanced training, I break down how you can easily create a system for this. It takes effort to do so, but it's a lot easier than you might think.

RESPECT THE CULTURE OF THE PLATFORM

When you distribute your content at scale across different platforms, you'll need to understand one thing very well: the culture of the platform!

Paul said it very well in 1 Corinthians 9: 19-23:

"For though I am free from all men, I have made myself a servant to all, that I might win the more; and to the Jews I became as a Jew, that I might win Jews; to those who are under the law, as under the law, that I might win those who are under the law; to those who are without law, as without law (not being without law toward God, but under law toward Christ), that I might win those who are without law; to the weak I became as weak, that I might win the weak. I have become all things to all men, that I might by all means save some. Now this I do for the gospel's sake, that I may be partaker of it with you."

Paul wanted to serve all men. In order to do so, he became all things to all men. He adapted himself depending on his audience. The same is true for us. Each social platform has its own culture—its own "language"; its own code of ethics. You simply have to respect this in order to be compatible, relevant, and received by your target audience. We can become all things to all men in order to win the people we're trying to reach.

DETERMINE YOUR BLUEPRINT

You need a blueprint. You need to create a schedule for each platform, and stick to it. Each platform is going to need a different posting frequency. For example, it's perfectly fine to post on Instagram and Facebook 3-5 times a day. However, you can't post 5 articles on your blog each day. If I'm sending out 3 emails each day, I'm going to do more harm than good.

Identify where your target audience is spending time, and determine a blueprint for your content distribution. In this blueprint you should have:

- The frequency by which you post
- What type of content you'll post
- What time of day (or week) you'll post

Once you have that in place, posting content will become a matter of filling in these blanks.

ALWAYS TALK BACK

When people engage with your content, make sure you're accessible. Remember, you're the expert. What better way to add value than allowing yourself to be accessible to your audience?

The more you distribute content on different platforms, and the more you add value, the more people will start "talking" to you by commenting, sharing and asking questions through direct messages. Make sure you always talk back. By doing so, you'll deepen and strengthen your relationship with your audience exponentially. The more thought you put into your replies, the more authentic your relationship with your audience will be.

Try to reply to as many comments as you can. If you simply have someone on your staff do all the replying, people will see through it. It's okay to get some help from time to time, but keep a pulse on your audience yourself. Don't try to shortcut the process: stay connected.

BE FLEXIBLE: ADOPT NEW PLATFORMS

Attention shifts all the time. Just because people spend time on Instagram today doesn't mean they will do the same tomorrow. With new technology and new ideas come new platforms. Change can happen fast. And when it happens, don't be afraid to let go of the old, so you can embrace the new.

Remember a little website called *myspace.com*? It used to be the biggest thing. Everyone who was anyone had a MySpace profile. Visit the site today, and it's merely an entertainment site with some mediocre content. Ask anyone 25 years or younger, and you'll find that they have never heard of MySpace!

Don't give blind loyalty to a platform. Email marketing is very different than it was five years ago. Uber changed the "transportation game" almost overnight (who takes a taxi these days?). Certain restaurants exist today solely because of UberEats, building their business off the platform Uber facilitates.

Always be on the lookout for new platforms that have the attention of the masses. Then, find a way to leverage that platform to connect to your target audience. Mobile apps would be nothing without the iPhone framework. Because of the iPhone, I can build an app that connects to the masses. Some of these apps have become platforms in and of themselves, such as Facebook, Instagram, Amazon, and YouTube.

What's next? What platforms are emerging that allow us to connect to our people? Where is the attention shifting? Cause when it shifts, it shifts quickly.

What about voice technologies like Alexa, Google Assistant, and Siri? How will we leverage this technology in the near future? As artificial intelligence and other technology emerges, let's keep our eyes and ears open. In the meantime, focus on where the attention is right now!

There are many tips and tricks to help you hit your brand message distribution out of the ballpark, but that goes beyond the scope of this chapter. In some of my more advanced training courses , I break down the process for you in detail, offering practical tools to build your branding machine.

If you haven't done any of this before, chances are all of this feels overwhelming and difficult. I promise you that it's not. It's a matter of embracing the current mindset—putting systems and structures in place that allow you to build momentum quickly.

We're living in an exciting time. The people we're trying to reach are accessible without a middleman. No broker or agent is needed as an in-between, no unsustainable fees involved. The world is at our fingertips. The internet has changed the game forever, and with new platforms being developed as we speak, we're just getting started.

CHAPTER 11

ADVERTISE

There are distinct differences between branding, advertising, and marketing. These three words are often used interchangeably, yet they are each unique.

Let me define the differences between the three.

BRANDING: YOUR STORY

Branding is all about who you are as an influencer. It's your story—your message. Branding is the very definition of the value you bring to your audience. That story will need to be told and demonstrated. In the previous chapter, we broke down some basic brand distribution strategies to do just that.

ADVERTISING: CREATING MOMENTS

Advertising is about creating a moment in front of your target audience. This moment is an opportunity for you to tell the story of your brand. It's the moment in time that you engage a new audience into what you have to offer.

MARKETING: THE CAMPAIGN

Marketing is the campaign that follows the moment. You can have the best advertising in the world, but if there's no process to follow the ad, the moment will remain isolated and render no return on investment. The campaign that follows the ad is a process designed to take a lead and turn them into a sale. The campaign is the process that finishes the job.

All three components are essential. You can't advertise without a clear story. You can't tell your story without creating moments to do so. You can't make a sale without a proper marketing campaign. Even if you had amazing marketing, you would still need leads to enter it in order to make sales (advertising). So none of these processes can be kept in isolation. All are dependent on one another.

We need an integrated approach: one that allows us to effectively create moments, tell our story, and convert attention into a process that sells product. Advertising serves as a conversion point that turns your audience's attention into a campaign (or funnel). While you're out there telling your story on all these platforms, you want there to be a moment when you convert that attention into this process. An effective ad allows you to do just that. When you create an ad, you should NEVER try to sell something. Always offer some sort of lead magnet that allows you to assimilate new leads.

Effective advertising will also reach and connect to new audiences that were previously not accessible to you. It develops an audience from scratch. Maybe you are an influencer, but you are wondering where to start. You have no database; no significant social media platforms; you have no audience whatsoever. If this is you, getting started may feel overwhelming. Don't be discouraged. Even the most successful influencers began with nothing. Some of the biggest influencers in the Bible started with absolutely no audience.

Remember John the Baptist? He was called by God to influence a nation. His message was to prepare a people for the coming of the Messiah. When he started, he had absolutely nobody listening to him. Let's read about it in the book of Matthew.

In those days John the Baptist came preaching in the wilderness of Judea, and saying, "Repent, for the kingdom of heaven is at hand!" For this is he who was spoken of by the prophet Isaiah, saying:

"The voice of one crying in the wilderness:
'Prepare the way of the Lord;
Make His paths straight.'"

Now John himself was clothed in camel's hair, with a leather belt around his waist; and his food was locusts and wild honey. Then Jerusalem, all Judea, and all the region around the Jordan went out to him and were baptized by him in the Jordan, confessing their sins. (Matthew 3:1-6)

John had a powerful message, given by God, with high value for the people of Israel. Yet he was in the wilderness of Judea, where no one could hear him. He didn't have a nice building in the good part of town where people knew to find him. No, John was the new kid on the block. Sure, people knew his dad, who was an established minister in the city; but John's message was so different that he had to start from scratch. He was, quite literally, a voice crying in the wilderness.

But God isn't intimidated by this. In fact, in Zechariah 4:10 He says:

> *Do not despise these small beginnings, for the Lord rejoices to see the work begin …*

Small beginnings are fine! God rejoices in the beginning of a new work. If we are faithful in the small things, He'll make us ruler over many things:

His lord said to him, 'Well done, good and faithful servant; you have been faithful over a few things, I will make you ruler over many things. (Matthew 25:23)

John knew this, and decided, against all odds, to start declaring his message where only a few could hear him. As he did so, something amazing happened.

Then Jerusalem, all Judea, and all the region around the Jordan went out to him … (Matthew 3:5)

God started to multiply John's ministry. The multitudes came to listen to him in a formerly undeveloped place—why? Because they were attracted to him. If we want to do something that has never been done before, we have to do so in undeveloped territory. New developments happen on the edge of chaos.

Effective advertising reaches an audience from an undeveloped place. Previously, this advertising was accessible only to those with serious means; those days are gone. We have a unique opportunity to bypass all major traditional media outlets and reach out to our target audiences directly. Here are some specific advantages we have that traditional advertising channels can't offer:

Measurability

How do you measure a magazine ad? How do you measure a TV ad? How do I know whether my featured ad in the newspaper really worked?

Well, you don't! Sure, there are minor things you can do to measure their success; but your options are limited. Most traditional media platforms seduce you with outrageous vanity metrics. Their true reach is significantly less than what they will promise you in their media kits.

Just because a TV channel reaches 8 million families in the US doesn't guarantee that anyone watches it if your programs run at 2:00 a.m. In addition, you don't know whether the person on the other side of the TV is actually interested in what you have to offer.

Digital advertising allows you to gain true metrics that cannot be manipulated. When you leverage digital platforms well, you will know who you're reaching. You'll know whether or not they are engaging with your ad; you can measure who purchased your product; you'll be able to re-target individuals who didn't engage; and much, much more.

Measurability isn't accessible through traditional advertising. Today, we have an advantage that allows us to measure just about everything.

Targeting

Most media platforms with the attention of the masses have an opportunity for you to advertise. Facebook, Instagram, YouTube, Google, and LinkedIn are just a few examples of platforms that let anyone advertise. It's a level playing field. You have the same opportunity as big corporations. Sure, you have less money to spend; but even $100 gets you started. The truth is, most large organizations are stuck on the traditional way of doing things, not realizing the opportunity new media brings to advertising.

Instead of broadcasting a one-size-fits-all commercial on national television, I can target my ads specifically to my audience. There's no guessing game when it comes to who may or may not see my ad. I know who will see it because I only distribute to people I want to reach.

If my product is gender specific, I can show my ad to only men or women. If my product is for people in a specific geographical area, I can make sure only those people see my ad. When I launch a product for a specific age group, I can make sure only that age group sees my ad. Some ads can even be targeted based on specific search history. For example, if someone searches "christian coaching certification" on Google, I can choose to deploy a pre-roll YouTube ad for my coaching certification program the next time this person watches any YouTube video. The opportunities are endless!

All of this can be done at a fraction of the price that traditional advertising requires.

Contextualization

The power of contextualization of your ads is grossly underestimated. Again, if you have an ad in a magazine, or on TV, you don't know who is reading or watching. You have to guess who is on the other side, and make your ad broad enough to speak to the largest possible audience.

A targeted ad through Facebook allows you to contextualize your copy, personalizing it to your target audience.

I can target Christian pastors in the greater Atlanta area who have expressed interest in leadership development resources. Instead of making my ad generic, I can have it say, "Thousands of Atlanta pastors have already discovered this incredibly effective leadership principle that has caused them to exponentially grow their churches!" I can even add an image of the Atlanta skyline, which will catch their attention if they're from that area. I can deploy countless instances of the same ad, targeted to pastors from different cities. All I need to do is to swap the graphic and the city name.

Contextualizing your ads is going to exponentially increase the return on investment.

Influencer Marketing

Advertising through new media platforms is only one way of getting in front of your target audience. Another way is through third-party influencers.

Chances are, there are countless influencers who already have the ability to reach an audience you are trying to reach yourself. By collaborating with these influencers, you'll be able to leverage their audience for your benefit.

I've leveraged others' influence over and over in a wide variety of projects. As a result, I've built massive databases for myself and my projects. This is not because I was strategically connected, but because the influencer with whom I collaborated was connected.

There are different ways you can approach influencer opportunities:

1. Cash in on emotional credit

If you're a relational person, chances are that you've built relationships with people over the years. Some of these people may have influence in a niche you are trying to target. Depending on the nature of the relationships that you have, you might be able to call in a favor. I've found that it never hurts to ask. They can always say no (which will happen at times). But sometimes they will say yes, and the results are amazing.

You have to make sure that when you call in a favor, you NEVER ask them to pitch your product. Nobody likes to pitch other people's products. Why would they? If they were going to pitch anybody's product, it would be their own.

When we talked about the perfect customer life cycle earlier in this book, we talked about bringing people into your proximity so you can further the conversation on your terms. We need to capture data in order to nurture our leads.

Whenever you call in a favor with anyone in your network, always offer something of value. If you develop a powerful lead magnet with high perceived value, you can offer it to someone else's audience. Then it doesn't come across like you're trying to sell something. All you have to do is to tell the influencer you've developed a resource that you believe his audience can benefit from, and that you are giving it away for free.

When you do it that way, you are not trying to sell. You are giving away value. The result is the same: people accessing the free resource become part of your campaign. Remember, if you can't give it away, you can't sell it!

Your influencer friends are less hesitant to send out your free resource than to sell your product. In fact, this will make your friend look good, because he's looking out for his audience by facilitating a resource that helps them.

2. Affiliate Relations

If an influencer doesn't want to do you a favor, he or she might be interested in an affiliate relationship. You can offer a generous percentage of commission over all sales made through the ad that the influencer allows you to push to their audience.

This may be a great way for the influencer to make significant money quickly. I've done this many times. It's an amazing win/win scenario that allows you to tap into an audience you don't have access to on your own. On the other hand, it allows the influencer to make money without doing anything other than giving you access.

There are different software solutions that track affiliate marketing results and calculate commission for you, completely hassle-free. As mentioned before, I'll provide you with a resource page at the end of the book, so you can check out some of these solutions for yourself.

3. Paying Influencers

Sometimes, it makes sense to simply pay an influencer to gain access to their audience. If you were going to spend money on ads anyway, you should consider this option.

In my experience, many influencers are willing to give you access to their audience at a relatively low price. They are honored you would pay them. Of course, you need to make sure you have a strong offer with a tested campaign before you do so; but once you're confident that your marketing campaign outputs the results you want, you can project whether or not paying an influencer is worth your money.

Before we end this chapter I want to remind you to NEVER try to sell something through your ad, unless it's re-marketing an offer you've already presented as part of your campaign.

Always offer value through an irresistible lead magnet. Give, don't ask. Ask later, when they are ready to buy. I'll share more about this in the next chapter, where we'll focusing on the marketing campaign.

CHAPTER 12

MARKETING

There are two kinds of people in this world:

1) People who run away from pain

2) People who run towards pleasure

It's really that simple. Most people are part of the first category. It's human nature. The majority of people don't necessarily know what they run towards, but they know one thing: they don't want the pain they're experiencing. Your message has the ability to remove some of these pain points. We simply must demonstrate that our information and services move people from pain to pleasure.

What I'm about to explain is a principle that should be at the foundation of every marketing campaign you will ever build. It's called "The Escape and Arrival Principle."

If I demonstrate how people can escape pain and arrive at a desired result, selling to them will be easy. Your campaign is really about engaging your audience in such a way that they start pursuing you for what you have, instead of you pursuing them. Sales, then, becomes the automatic by-product of an effective, well-developed campaign.

The Bible says in Psalm 9:9-10, "The Lord is a refuge for the oppressed, a stronghold in times of trouble."

"Oppression" and "trouble" are the things people are try to escape. A "refuge" and "stronghold" are the desired arrival points of the target audience of the Lord. The Lord's value proposition in this Scripture is that His message has the ability to move people from pain to pleasure.

Your campaign should be about helping people escape pain, and showing the path that leads them to desired results in their lives. If you can prove that your information will have the ability to do so, you will have an audience that is ready to buy from you.

In essence, that's how Jesus operated. He demonstrated His message in a powerful way, thus proving that what He possessed had to the ability to remove people's pain. Whether the pain point was sickness, oppression, or even death, Jesus demonstrated that His message worked.

THE NICODEMUS PRINCIPLE

In John 3:1-5, we read the following account of a man name Nicodemus:

> There was a man of the Pharisees named Nicodemus, a ruler of the Jews. This man came to Jesus by night and said to Him, "Rabbi, we know that You are a teacher come from God; for no one can do these signs that You do unless God is with him."

Jesus answered and said to him, "Most assuredly, I say to you, unless one is born again, he cannot see the kingdom of God."
Nicodemus said to Him, "How can a man be born when he is old? Can he enter a second time into his mother's womb and be born?"
Jesus answered, "Most assuredly, I say to you, unless one is born of water and the Spirit, he cannot enter the kingdom of God.

This is a well-known portion of scripture. We've adopted it into our core theology, using it to illustrate the gospel message as we explain to people the need to be born again. The interesting part is that Jesus was never proactively preaching here. He wasn't on a pulpit in front of the multitudes. In fact, He was fast asleep in the middle of the night when Nicodemus came to pay him a visit in obscurity.

It's the ultimate example of what true engagement accomplishes. Jesus didn't pursue nor ask Nicodemus to come to his house. Nicodemus pursued Jesus. When nobody was watching, when nobody was listening, Nicodemus snuck out of his house to pursue Jesus for answers to his questions. Jesus didn't try to "sell" Nicodemus the gospel message until Nicodemus pursued Him.

In verse 1, Nicodemus says, "Rabbi, we know that You are a teacher come from God; for no one can do these signs that You do unless God is with him." What triggered Nicodemus to pursue Jesus? It was the value Jesus demonstrated. It was the signs He gave His audience, proving His message was backed by the kingdom of God. This demonstration became the catalyst for Nicodemus. He basically asks Jesus, "How do I get what you have?" In answer, Jesus shows him the pathway to the Kingdom.

We can learn a lot from this story as it relates to marketing. Demonstrate before you ask! Give before you sell! When you do so, people will ask for more of what you have, which makes your sale easier. In fact, the sale will become the byproduct of the process you've just demonstrated.

THE ESCAPE AND ARRIVAL PRINCIPLE

When I broke down the perfect customer lifecycle into seven phases, I explained lead magnets in detail. This is where your marketing starts: delivering a powerful, valuable lead magnet allows you to demonstrate the benefit you bring to your target audience. A lead magnet is designed to show people you can help them escape pain and experience desired results.

Let's break down the escape and arrival principle in a graphic.

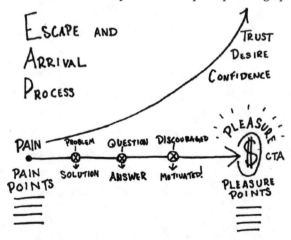

Let's say you're trying to sell a leadership development program that helps leaders succeed and bring their organization to the next level.

The left side represents the many pain points leaders experience, such as:

- Financial struggles
- Delegation challenges
- Hiring the wrong people
- Poor time management
- Conflict
- Toxic organization culture
- Lack of capacity to grow
- Depression
- Lack of vision
- Etc.

On the right side, we have the outcomes we know these people want, such as:

- Financial stability and abundance
- A well-oiled team
- The right players in the right places
- Optimized productivity
- Peace in the organization
- A healthy culture
- Systems and structures to scale their organizations for growth
- Joy
- Vision
- Etc.

If my lead magnet proves to my target audience that it moves them from the left side of the graph to the right side, there will be a curved line that goes up, as represented in this graph.

How do I demonstrate this shift to my audience?

1) Identify with Their Struggles

If I show my audience that I understand what they're going through, it creates a connection. If I enter the conversation they're already having with themselves, I'll establish be able to further that conversation. Then, I convince them I know what they're going through, which allows me to take them on a journey to escape the negatives in their lives.

2) Paint the Picture of the External Struggle

I need to paint a picture of what I, personally, went through, in such a way that it connects to their situation. For example, I can say something like this:

"I remember being a pastor of a small, struggling church. We had just purchased our first permanent venue. It was a leap of faith, as we were struggling each day to make ends meet. Shortly after this, conflict with one of my elders caused turmoil in the congregation that resulted in one-third of the families leaving the church. To say this was a financial disaster was an understatement. How were we ever going to pay the mortgage?"

In this example, I'm showing them the external forces coming against me, which resulted in the pain I experienced. I'm showing my target audience that I understand what they're going through.

3) Paint the Picture of the Internal Struggle

This is where we make the narrative personal. We shift from external forces to the forces within me that come against me. Here's is an example of what that could look like:

"I hadn't slept for days. The thought of having to preach on Sunday morning paralyzed me. I couldn't do it. It was only two months ago that I'd stood in front of the congregation, declaring, full of faith, how God was going to provide funds for this new building. And now, just weeks later, I felt defeated. I was ashamed. I promised the people something I knew I could no longer deliver on. The stress I was under caused me to hyperventilate at times ..."

You get the point. By hearing your the internal struggle, your audience will feel that they are not alone in their own situations.

4) Show Them the Epiphany

This is the turning point you experienced in your life that allowed you to turn your situation around for the better. The purpose of including this moment is to show your audience there is hope—a way out. It may sound something like this:

"I finally decided this was it. The pressure had broken me to the point where I'd told my wife that we had to close the church. I couldn't bear it any longer. I drafted up a statement to read at church in the morning. Then, something amazing happened. I was lying in bed and suddenly had an epiphany that I'd never had before. This epiphany was seemingly insignificant, but would change the trajectory of my life as a leader. Looking back now, I can't believe I never saw this before. Had I seen this new

revelation earlier, it would have saved me so much trouble. I
ripped up my statement, and with my newfound insight, I was
excited to stand in front of the congregation...."

See how I took people on a journey from depression to hope,
where they can actually believe that there is a way out? If I got out,
they reason, then they can, too.

Once your campaign takes them to a place of hope, it's time to
demonstrate the power of your message. In the graph, you'll see three
key moments that move your target audience from pain to pleasure. I
choose three, but it can be any number you see fit for your campaign.
I've broken it down into three distinct types of demonstrations that
allow you to keep moving your audience from left to right, and for
the curved line to go up.

Each of the circles on the line represent an "inception moment."
These are basically mini experiences, where your target audience sam-
ples what you have to offer.

Let's say the three "stops" on the line at the bottom are part of a
three-part video course that helps leaders succeed. Maybe the video
course is called "The Three Mistakes That Will Keep You Stuck!" You
can create a three-part training that moves people from pain to pleasure. Here are three different ways you can do this:

Question and Answer

If you identify with a question you know your target audience is
asking, and answer that question for them, you'll move them from
left to right.

Problem and Solution

If you identify with a problem you know your target audience has, and solve it for them with no strings attached, you will move them from pain to pleasure even more!

Depression to Encouragement

If you identify with the depression or negative feelings your target audience is experiencing, and give them encouragement through hope, you'll move them towards pleasure even more.

These are just three ways you can demonstrate your message to your target audience.

In the process, you'll create a curved line in the graph. This represents:

Trust, in you as the expert

Desire, for more of what they've just tasted

Confidence, that they can actually succeed

If we execute this correctly, we create a situation where our campaign pushes the audience to a high in all three areas as they move from pain to pleasure. Subconsciously, your prospect will start begging you for more where that came from, which makes a sale merely a formality.

When, at the end of the process, I present my audience with an opportunity to get more of what they just experienced, they easily say yes. That's the purpose of your campaign: Engaging your audience in a way that makes your call to action easy: the "natural next step."

DYNAMIC RESPONSE COMMUNICATION

In order to maximize your engagement, we need Dynamic Response Communication. This systematically moves people through all seven phases of the perfect customer life cycle, which we discussed in chapter six.

Each phase of the life cycle has its own goal. Unless that goal is reached, there is no reason to further the conversation to the next phase. Dynamic Response Communication interacts with your target audience based on their engagement (or non-engagement). In other words, the next communication piece is determined by how your recipient interacted with the previous communication piece.

Let's say you've offered a free training course on how to manage one's time. The training promises that if the prospect follows the course, they'll get double the work done in half the time. You've given this course away to your audience, so you engage and hopefully, sell a comprehensive, premium time-management course guaranteed to change their lives.

In chapter six, we identified that phase two of the customer life cycle is "capturing" your traffic into your database. Once you've brought your audience into proximity, you can engage and nurture them. The goal of phase three is engagement—needed to make the sale. But engagement is only going to happen if they've consumed your content.

Just because they asked for your course doesn't mean they will actually consume that content. You'd be surprised how many people request a lead magnet, but proceed to do absolutely nothing with it.

In fact, more than 50% of all resources requested are not going to be consumed—*unless* you use dynamic response communication.

Dynamic Response Communication ensures you that you are reaching your goal for each phase before continuing to move your audience to the next goal. It allows you to create a contingency plan, in case your previous communication failed to move your prospect deeper into your sales cycle.

When someone requests your lead magnet, it's crucial that your prospect actually consumes that content. In order to make certain this happens, you want to have mechanisms in place that detect whether the person has consumed it. If someone requests your time management course, you want to know that they actually accessed the course.

If they didn't, you want to follow up accordingly. If they did, you would want to follow up accordingly too. A contingency plan might look like this:

As you can see, there are multiple communication assets that are part of the sequence. When I say "communication assets," I don't just mean emails. These can be text messages, voice messages, direct mail pieces, or even custom video communications.

Each phase has a goal. In our example, the goal is "lead magnet consumption." So when people request my lead magnet, they are going to get an email that delivers the lead magnet. If they fail to access the course in a timely manner, we want our contingency plan to kick in.

Our contingency plan, in this example, is email number two in the sequence. This email is sent automatically, in the event that the prospect hasn't accessed my course. The email reminds him that the course is still waiting for him, and reinforces the value proposition of what the course will do for him.

If this reminder doesn't do the trick, there's another backup plan that can be triggered. You can have as many or as few contingency plans as you like. Depending on the data points you have captured, you can get creative in how you follow up on this prospect, until he or she accesses the material.

Once your prospect goes through the course, your contingency is no longer needed; the goal for that phase has been reached. The system now takes people out of the sequence, and skips all other backup communication assets. This lead is automatically moved to the next phase in your cycle.

I know that this sounds complicated. It truly isn't. There is software available that manages all your dynamic response interaction. If you visit *unleashedforimpact.com/toolbox*, I give you access to my personal toolbox. In that toolbox, you'll see different solutions I use for different purposes. I'll give you pros and cons of each, as well as recommendations on when to use each solution.

Software is easy. Everyone can learn it. It just takes some time and focus to do so.

CREATING AN INDIVIDUAL UNIVERSE

One-size-fits-all communication doesn't work. Traditional online communication is all about sending the same message to all people at the one time. This creates disconnects. Too many of these disconnects, and people stop listening.

For example, your traditional model of communication is that, on Monday morning you send out your ministry newsletter. That's just what you do, right? Your newsletter goes out to all members of your mailing list, regardless of who they are in relationship to you. It doesn't matter whether or not people have been connected to you for years, or just came into your database last week. They get the same communication. The problem is that one size does not fit all.

One-size-fits-all communication is always based on the assumption that what I'm saying is relevant to you. The truth is that there are certain things I don't want to tell you if you were a first time visitor in my church last week, but that I do want to tell members who have been faithful for many years. There are things you want to tell the women in your church, but not the men. When an email in my inbox doesn't apply to me, it ultimately causes me to unsubscribe (or ignore your emails all together).

What we want is tailored communication, relevant to both horizontal as well as vertical segmentations of my audience. Horizontal segmentation is based on my target demographics such as gender, age, occupation, organization size, family situation, income level, and so on. Vertical segmentation is based on how deep the person is in my sales cycle—what phase of the perfect customer life cycle they're in, and what communication they need to move closer to the goal.

Again, there is software that manages all of this. It keeps track of who is where, and communicates the next logical step in the process. This ensures your communication is always on point, always relevant, and always in line with where people are.

As a result, you create an individual universe for each person in your marketing process. The path each individual takes is going to be different. A thousand leads may come in through the same offer, but after a few days, they are all immersed into their own individual realities, depending on how they engaged with your content.

In some of my more advanced training, I walk you through implementing this strategy in your organization. There is so much to say about an effective marketing process. In this book, we're only scratching the surface of what can be done.

IT'S NOT ABOUT LIST SIZE

Before we close off this chapter, I want to mention something. Even though the size of your database matters, it's not the most important thing. I've seen massive databases that absolutely did nothing for the organization's bottom line. I've also seen emails lists of just a few hundred names perform like crazy. Why? Because those few hundred people were engaged!

Engagement is the launchpad for every product. If you get it right, even a small audience can generate hundreds of thousands of dollars. Yes, this will require creativity, focus, and effort, but it it's possible. I've seen it over and over again.

My online training breaks down several engagement campaigns that I've personally run—campaigns that converted a small list of engaged people into raving fans who spent thousands of dollars. Check out the back of the book for more information about those resources.

CHAPTER 13

SELL

This chapter, and the next one, are a bit shorter. I decided it was important to give a bit of attention to these two topics.

We've already discussed phase four in the perfect customer life cycle: selling to your prospect. This process involves a psychological aspect as well as a technical aspect. Throughout this book, we've already focused on several psychological aspects of the sales cycle. In this chapter, I want to briefly touch on the technical process of how to effectively sell your product.

How do you make an online transaction? How do you fully integrate the strategy and process you've developed? In this chapter, I'll give you practical advice on how to make sales online. Putting the right mechanisms in place can be overwhelming if you've never done it. A simple search on " ways to sell stuff online" gives you a wide variety of options. How do you know which solutions are best for you?

Below are my thoughts on selecting selling mechanisms for your campaign. Not every solution out there is good. As a matter of fact, many online sales solutions have major limitations that keep you from implementing the strategies in this book. Honestly, this topic is very huge. Here are some guidelines to help you navigate it.

USE SALES FUNNELS

It's important to understand what a sales funnel is, and how it differs from a traditional website.

A traditional website is horizontally organized: you can access information through a navigation menu structure. You hop from one page another. A good website allows you to find out about the company and the products they're selling. The disadvantage of this approach is that you give control to the visitor on how they want to engage with you. You're basically telling them, "Here's a menu; figure out what you want," instead of guiding them where you want them to go.

A sales funnel does exactly that. There is no page navigation. A sales funnel is a one-dimensional page with a singular objective and call to action. This call to action is reasonable enough (with a low threshold) to have a good chance of being answered by the prospect. Once a call to action is answered, this person moves deeper into the funnel. A page is revealed that's only shown to those who've answered the previous call to action.

A sales funnel is more of a three-dimensional website, that allows a prospect to move deeper into the sales cycles by taking micro-steps forward into the funnel. The graphic below illustrates the difference between the two strategies.

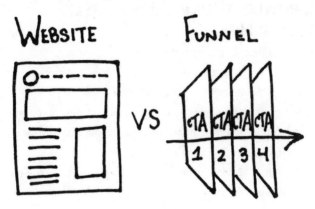

The next webpage is only revealed if the prospect has proven ready for the information and call to action. Remember the ascending value ladder? A sales funnel allows you to deploy a mechanism to move people into higher levels of financial engagement, instead of offering all the "options" or "products" on one page.

Now, depending on what you're selling, a traditional shopping cart website might be a good solution. If you're a clothing brand or other catalog-based business, it's probably a good idea to go that route. But, in my experience, any type of content-driven product is more effectively sold through strategic, intentionally-developed sales funnels.

Again, there are multiple great software solutions that help you to do this effectively. My toolbox at *unleashedforimpact.com/toolbox* shows you a list of options, and my advanced training works through each option in much more detail.

THE POWER OF ONE-CLICK UPSELL MECHANISMS

The ascending value ladder serves multiple purposes:

It allows you to ease in prospects by offering something cheap, before asking them to buy higher priced products.

Once a prospects engages with a cheap offer, it allows you to move them into higher levels of financial engagement with just one click. This is called a "one click upsell."

When someone buys something cheap, you capture their credit card. You don't have to ask for it again. You want to make it as easy as possible. Obviously, you want your customer's permission to charge them, but you want to make the purchase process as seamless and effortless as possible. Because I already captured the credit card on my cheap product, I can offer a secondary product on the confirmation page that allows me to charge the card with just one click, if the customer chooses to "add that product to their cart."

The easy nature of the one-click upsell causes the conversion rate to boost. Nobody likes to type in a long credit card number. Asking them to do it twice creates friction in the sales process and therefore reduces your conversion rate.

Most shopping carts won't allow you to do one-click upsells. Make sure your cart allows you to do this. It will make your sales funnel far more effective.

SUBSCRIPTIONS ARE THE BEST

Make sure you always have a subscription product as part of your product portfolio. Subscriptions allow you to build monthly cash flow like no other type of product, because you know that every month (or year), your subscription automatically renews and collects money on your behalf. If you're selling subscriptions, all you have to do is add more subscriptions each month than the number of cancellations. It's a beautiful thing.

Not every shopping cart lets you run subscriptions. Before you pick a solution, make sure subscriptions are part of the features of that specific solution.

OFFER PAYPAL

If you can, offer PayPal as a secondary payment option. PayPal has proven to increase sales conversion rates by over 10%. If you're a PayPal user, you know that it keeps you from having to pull out your credit card to pay. You simply click the PayPal option and finish the transaction within seconds. This will make the transaction friction-free for a good percentage of your clients.

Please note that PayPal does not replace your normal credit card payment option. It needs to be added as an additional option. Replacing it will actually have the opposite effect, because the majority of your clients prefer to pay by credit card. Offering an alternative simply increases your conversion rate enough to make it worth the effort.

INTEGRATION WITH YOUR COMMUNICATION ENGINE

Phase four in your perfect customer life cycle is to sell. This means the goal associated for this phase is to make an actual transaction. Based on what we just learned about dynamic response communication, it's important for your marketing engine to "know" when a sale is made.

Nothing is as awkward as a marketing email that is trying to sell you something you already bought yesterday. You want your marketing communication to be tailored to whether or not someone actually bought something. You want your contingency plan to stop the moment the sales goal is reached. In order to do so, your shopping cart will need to talk to your marketing engine, so that the campaign can stop at the right time.

Most shopping cart solutions don't have this capability. Yet you can't market with confidence unless you have this assurance. You want tailored communication, on par with both your prospect's engagement as well as their buying.

Note: Sometimes a shopping cart is not natively compatible with your marketing software. There may be a third party plugin that builds that connection for you. Check out my toolbox at *unleashedforimpact.com/toolbox* for more information.

MY PET PEEVE

This is something I've seen over and over again...it's a real pet peeve of mine: Back office processes that control your sales and marketing!

The bigger the organization, the more standardized processes you're going to have:

- Existing software
- Existing sales processes
- Existing habits and routines
- Existing staff members who have been doing certain things a certain way for a very long time

If you're organization is fairly large chances are you have a lot of red tape that slows you down. In fact, red tape is the primary reason we don't innovate.

I remember working with a new client not too long ago. This client wanted me to help innovate both their product portfolio as well as their sales and marketing process. I consulted with them for one full day, which resulted in a clear, focused strategy. I told them that, if they followed my lead, this strategy would help them generate $200K in just five weeks. I showed them the steps, the process, the strategy, and the execution plan. I was happily surprised when they followed my lead and did exactly what I told them they should do. Guess what? They didn't make $200K. No, they made $250K instead. Amazing results!

We then took that strategy and moved it into the second phase. We did another marketing push, which increased their revenues to $400K in the weeks to follow. This was an incredible success. $400K in product sales was roughly a 3000% increase in their revenue.

But then...it happened! The back office processes weren't able to manage the new sales data in the old way any longer. As a result, the red tape began to dictate the marketing and sales process. Because the shopping cart didn't communicate properly with the existing database, this client decided to change shopping carts without consulting me. We were using the cart system I'd put in place for intentional reasons—it allowed me to do things that contributed to the success. Now, I was no longer able to do those things.

Our dynamic response communication was cut off for lack of integration. This threw off my messaging with my prospects. Long story short, the "magic" that once created the success was suffocated overnight by back office processes. Not only did the revenue stream virtually stop, but the expenses of this mistake were tremendous.

My point is that innovation requires change. Change is hard. However, if you always do what you've always done, you'll always get what you've always gotten!

Have the courage to change your back office processes and align them with what works. I promise you, if you want to see success, you need to be willing to change how you run your organization.

Remember this:

"The reasonable man adapts himself to the world; the unreasonable one persists in trying to adapt the world to himself. Therefore, all progress depends on the unreasonable man."

—*George Bernard Shaw*

Don't let the past control you. Be unreasonable!

CHAPTER 14

DELIVER YOUR PRODUCT

It's one thing to sell; it's another thing to effectively deliver your product. In delivering product there are two main things to ensure you do:

1) Wow your customer as explained in Chapter 6.

2) Ensure a seamless customer experience.

Wowing your customer is important for reasons we've already discussed. The Bible says in Luke 6:29, "And from him who takes away your cloak, do not withhold your tunic either." This example is about someone taking something that they didn't pay for. Luke teaches that, when this happens, you should add to what they took by giving more. How much more should we give to those who pay for something! We should always overdeliver. Sweeten the deal. Give more than what we promised. This gives us leverage.

Delivering the goods in a seamless way is equally important. How frustrating it is to buy something and have a delivery process that's user *un*friendly. It's one thing to sell a book and ship it; it's another thing to deliver an online course or an educational program.

There are certain things you must think through when you decide to sell and deliver content. Like your shopping cart, you need to know what delivery options you're looking for before you blindly adopt a platform. Once you pick a platform, it's hard to go back.

What's the best way to ship a package? How do you deliver an online course? A masterclass? A twelve month training program? Maybe you're trying to sell recordings of a conference you did. For each product, the question is the same: "How do I get this to my customer in a user-friendly way that doesn't allow others to steal my stuff?"

Without spending too much time on this, let me give you some suggestions. Once a sale is made, the danger is to forget about the customer experience that follows the sale. However, it's much easier to turn a customer into a repeat customer than it is to find a brand new one. A repeat customer is only created if we pay attention to the process of delivery. Here are some practical delivery tips to help you think through your mechanisms.

SHIPPING PACKAGES

When someone buys a physical product from you, like a book, you're required to ship the item to the customer. To make the experience for the customer great, there are several things you should do:

Keep the customer in the loop by setting the expectation. Make sure that your order confirmation is clear as far as when the customer can expect their purchase.

If possible, provide them with tracking information.

Provide them with your contact information. People want an effective way to contact you with a quick response time. If you don't provide that, you'll end up frustrating clients, incurring charge-backs, and losing customers.

Pay attention to your packaging. There are cost effective ways to make it stick out from the competition. Custom boxes, envelopes, and packing materials grab people's attention.

Do something extra. Put something in the package that they didn't purchase. Most companies have dead inventory of product, or items that won't break the bank to give away. Add something extra with a short note that explains the item goes a long way.

These are just some ideas for how you can deliver a physical package in a way that wows the customer.

DIGITAL CONTENT

When you're delivering a digital product, the process needs to be user-friendly. I've purchased digital products in the past from companies that were user *un*friendly way. Too many times, we make things confusing and unintuitive.

Here are some things you need to consider as you're delivering digital content:

1) Delivery Automation

You want to automate as much of the process as possible after the sale. You don't want to manually create accounts on a different platform. At first, this may seem no big deal; but I promise you, it won't be scalable over time. Any delay you cause in your sale-to-delivery process will cause friction and frustration for the client. Make sure your sales and delivery processes are integrated, so your customer's experience is seamless, simple, and user-friendly.

2) Pick Your Platform Accordingly

Depending on your product, you'll need certain capabilities in your delivery platform. As you're designing your product and picking your platform, here are some formats to think through. In my toolbox at *unleashedforimpact.com/toolbox,* I listing different platforms you can consider for different products.

The best thing to do is to pick a diverse platform that allows for multiple product formats. This will help you avoid having to adopt multiple platforms and multiple monthly subscription fees that can really add up if you're not careful.

3) Drip Content

Drip content is ideal if you have an evergreen, progressive digital product that rolls out over a period of time. For example, if you have a 12-week course to sell, you probably want to drip your content weekly into your customers' user accounts.

Practically, this means the course unlocks new content every single week until the customer completes the 12 weeks. It doesn't matter when the client buys the course: someone who buys today will log in to see only Week 1 content in their account, whereas someone who bought the course three weeks ago will see three weeks of content. Everybody is on their own schedule.

4) Progressive Course Content

Progressive course content is similar to drip content, however it's different in one respect: The content is not dripped based on timers, but "opened up." Clients progress in the course, and the completion of one lesson automatically opens the next lesson. In this scenario, a "student" determines how fast he or she completes the course.

In some cases, of course, it does not make sense to progressively deliver content, and I may be better to drip it with set delays. Let's say you are creating that 12-week course, but you don't have all the content. You only have content for Weeks 1 and 2. By making your content drip, you're buying yourself time to produce more material before the timer unlocks those modules.

Again, it's all about what you decide is best for your product, audience, and situation.

5) Archived Content

Maybe your product is ideal for archived content. Archived content is much like the Netflix model, where you create an environment with a wide variety of content items available on demand. A client simply logs in and chooses what they want to access.

I work with many churches who love to create portal environments like this to archive their sermons. The portal becomes an ever-growing pool of content, organized by category, that allows users to access anything they want at any time.

6) Assessments and Quizzes

Does your product include assessments and quizzes? Sometimes you need the ability to "test" your students to validate their progress in your program. In that case, your platform needs to have the ability to assess the user.

Think this through before you choose your platform. Once you've picked one, you don't want to switch.

7) Live Content

How do you deliver live content? Maybe you have a "coaching program" that requires you to engage with a live audience. There are plenty of software solutions that allow you to deliver live content; however, not all of them will be compatible with your other platforms. Do your homework before you pick, and save yourself a lot of frustration. In my toolbox at u*nleashedforimpact.com/toolbox* you'll find a full overview of platforms I've used in the past, personal notes, and pros and cons for each of them.

8) A Secure Portal

Make sure your content is delivered securely. Don't just send a public link for everyone to access. This is not only unprofessional, but also not smart. If people feel the content they just paid for is accessible to the whole world, it devalues their perception of the product—and you.

I know it's tempting to shortcut the process, but I promise that in the long run, it won't work to your advantage. Spend the extra time and money to do it right.

These are just some points to consider as you work through your delivery strategy. There are many more things you could think about, but I want to get your mind in the right place before you plan. I hope these touch points help you strategize well.

CHAPTER 15

WHAT DO I DO NEXT?

Throughout the last fourteen chapters, I've given you an overview of what I've learned over the years. This book is by no means a complete catalogue of lessons; but I hope it has given you divine inspiration you to bring your God-given message to the market. I also hope this book has provided practical insight on how to steward your message, reach more people, and leave a deeper impact.

You may be feeling overwhelmed by the principles and information we've discussed. It's true that there are many moving parts. The truth, however, is that everyone can do this. You don't have to have some special skill set. You'll find that it's a lot easier than you think. Everything in this book is simple, but that doesn't mean it will be easy. It will require commitment, perseverance, and hard work. Seeing something significant become a reality requires energy, after all.

The good news is that you don't have to do it alone. In some of my more advanced training, I will answer the questions you might be asking right now. I'll also point you to the right tools for your situation.

When I started my journey, I knew absolutely nothing. Nobody told me how to do this. I learned through trial and error. You don't have to struggle as much as I did. You can save you a lot of time, energy, frustration, and money if you allow me to walk you through this.

As we're wrapping up this book, I want to reinforce one final thought:

You are unique. Your message is unique. What you bring to the table is new. Therefore, you are an innovator. There is no other point of reference for what you have. God gave you a gift that was uniquely picked out by Him for you.

Because it's new, it will shape the future. It will disrupt the status quo. The past does not facilitate an environment that can hold what you bring into the future.

Don't be afraid for pushback. Don't be afraid of disruption and opposition. Don't be surprised when you rattle the cage of the establishment. Be bold. Be strong. Be everything God created you to be. Together, we can change history, impact people, and make the world a better place!

You have been given a message! Let's make sure it gets to where it needs to go. Together, we can do this. Apply the principles learned to unleash your message, reach more people and produce blessing for others as well as yourself.

Become unleashed!